EAR

A space adventure g

⛵

This Armada book belongs to:

Liam Sammon

6 Shallwell

Drive Norfolk

EARTH BRAIN

A space adventure gamebook

Keith Faulkner
Illustrated by Peter Joyce

An Armada Original

Earthbrain was first published in Armada in 1987.

Armada is an imprint of the Children's Division,
part of the Collins Publishing Group,
8 Grafton Street, London W1X 3LA.

Printed in Great Britain by
Wm. Collins Sons & Co. Ltd, Glasgow.

EARTHBRAIN

This is a gamebook: a mixture of story and puzzles which you must solve. It is not read as an ordinary book but section by section according to the instructions given in italics at the end of each section. Sometimes you will be offered a choice of sections to turn to next. It is generally a good idea to keep a note of where you've been and to help you do this there are Tracking Sheets printed at the end of this book.

All you need to play this book is a pencil and some paper. And your brains! Good luck!

EARTHBRAIN

You are about to set off on a mind-boggling adventure taking you out into the wild uncharted regions of deep space. On this mission you will need to use your wits, not your weapons.

However, you shall not be sent off into space completely empty-handed so choose ten items from the list below to help you on your journey.

This list contains all the things that any sensible adventure-hunter would not be without. So, choose the ten items carefully and tick the boxes.

You never know – your life may depend on your choice . . .

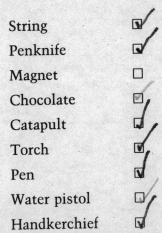

String

Penknife

Magnet

Chocolate

Catapult

Torch

Pen

Water pistol

Handkerchief

Compass ☑

Elastic bands ☑

Superglue ☐

Peashooter ☑

Clockwork mouse ☐

Calculator ☑

Chalk ☐

Magnifying glass ☑

Chewing gum ☐

Rubber spider ☐

Marbles ☑

Spud gun ☑

EARTHBRAIN

Professor Wopplebanger was sitting in his favourite armchair doing very, very difficult sums in his head – just for fun.

He did difficult sums in his head to help him relax after doing extremely difficult sums all day at work. The only problem was that no one ever knew whether his answers were correct, unless they happened to have a huge computer to check them.

Professor Wopplebanger was probably the cleverest person in the whole world. But, although he knew almost everything there was to know, there was one thing he didn't know. He was completely unaware of what was happening fifty miles above his very brainy head.

For there hovered a large spacecraft.

It didn't look like a spacecraft. In fact, it looked more like a large, pink washing machine. But, as washing machines seldom hover fifty miles above the earth and are never, never made in pink, it was most probably a spacecraft.

Hanging beneath it was a rather strange device with lots of tubes, wires and fiddly bits connected to a nozzle which pointed straight down.

To be more accurate, it pointed straight down at the bald, shiny, but extremely brainy head of Professor Wopplebanger.

Inside the spacecraft an alien voice warbled, "Activate the transporter beam," Then a hand with rather too many fingers that looked like it was wearing a slightly tatty, yellow rubber glove, reached for a shiny, red lever.

Now, anyone can make a mistake, even a mega-intelligent interstellar life-form.

For at that very moment forty-five miles below, a jumbo jet changed course. It changed course to avoid a flock of migrating geese, not because the pilot particularly liked geese but simply because he didn't want to spend hours at the airport, picking bits of roast goose out of his jet engines.

Then everything happened very quickly . . .

The lever was pulled. A beam of something odd shot down towards the earth, bounced off the jumbo jet, zoomed off at an angle, went straight through the roof of a house, just missed the cat, and then hit YOU . . .

As it's unlikely that you've been hit by a transporter beam before, perhaps I should tell you how they work.

To put it simply, they break up your body into very small bits called atoms. Then they suck all these atoms back up the beam and put you back together again at the top, hopefully in roughly the same arrangement.

This accounts for the fact that it's always easy to tell if you're on a planet where transporter beams are popular because there are so many people walking about with noses and ears in very peculiar places.

However, I don't want to worry you. It's not really as dangerous as it sounds, especially if the transporter has been regularly serviced.

So cross your fingers, hope that they're still in the right place at the other end of the beam, and turn to **52**.

1

"That is correct," says RU12. There's a whirring sound as the droid tries in vain to rearrange his facial components into something resembling a smile of triumph.

"We are now ready to begin the transfer of your brainpower into my computer matrixes." You squirm as he lowers a plastic dome over your head and begins to fix the adhesive electrodes.

If you are carrying some superglue, turn to 23.
If not, turn to 162.

2

The ship is spinning faster and faster as it approaches the swirling vortex of the black hole. You remember reading that a black hole can contain entire planets, all squeezed into a piece of matter no bigger than a pea.

Oh, dear, what an end to an adventure, you think, as you begin to shrink . . .

Well, Earthbrain, this is the end. You may have failed this time, but you can always try again. Who knows what strange beings you might meet on your next adventure . . .

3

You slip silently into the docking bay, Psili's yellow foot flapping softly behind. You spot his ship amongst the many vehicles at the far end of the vast chamber. As you begin to creep forward you suddenly freeze as several huge guard droids come into view.

"We must find a way to distract them," says Psili, gesturing towards a control terminal on the wall. "If we could set off the alarm system, perhaps we might be able to reach the ship during the confusion," he adds.

As you approach the terminal you see a display panel headed ALARM CODE. You must work out the code and decide which button to press.

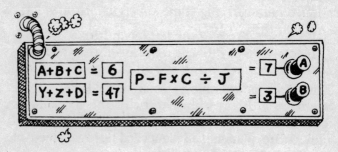

If you want to press button A, turn to **66**.
If you want to press button B, turn to **121**.

4

"That's most useful," says Psili, entering this valuable information into the data bank.

"Why did you want to know?" you enquire.

"Well," begins Psili, "we've been monitoring Earth broadcasts for some time and we heard this question asked in a political debate yet, with all our computer resources, we were unable to answer it."

At that moment an alarm starts to wail. Psili leaps to his foot. "Quick, action stations, we're being attacked!"

On the screen you see a vast shape approaching rapidly, its front end opening up like an enormous gaping mouth. Psili, hopping to the controls, trips over Hoover and falls in a wobbly, yellow heap.

"Hurry," he cries, "pull the starboard control lever, quickly." You rush to the controls. There are three gleaming levers, one on the left, one on the right and one in the middle. But which one should you pull?

*If you want to pull the left lever, turn to **21**.*
*If you want to pull the right lever, turn to **163**.*
*If you want to pull the middle lever, turn to **90**.*

5

Just as you're about to test the circuit, a messenger bursts into the room.

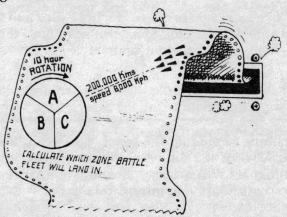

"Our scanners have just detected a large battle fleet approaching Gargul," he cries, thrusting a printout into your hand. "But we can't really tell where it's going to land."

Looking at the printout, you turn to Psili. "We must calculate where RU12 is landing or we'll never be prepared in time."

*If you think he'll land in zone A, turn to **191**.*
*If you think he'll land in zone B, turn to **216**.*
*If you think he'll land in zone C, turn to **209**.*

6

It's now completely black. You feel your way forwards along the smooth shaft. Suddenly you are falling and you slide downwards until you emerge with a bump. Looking round, you find yourself face to face with a very startled Psili.

"Where are we?" you ask, hoping for a pleasant surprise.

"We're locked up in a cell," replies Psili, "and I'm not sure what's going to happen next, but I think it's likely to be rather uncomfortable."

*Turn to **55**.*

7

Straining to see into the green, gloomy shadows, you look for the source of the movement. What could it be? What's been following you? Are those eyes, or is it just your imagination?

If you can't see anything, turn to **43**.
If you can see four faces, turn to **72**.
If you can see six faces, turn to **37**.

8

You are soon joined by Psili, back in your quarters. "Do you really think we can defend ourselves against the droids, Earthbrain?" he asks.

You tell Psili that in computer studies, back on Earth, you had once blown up one of the school computers by causing it to overload its circuits. "The droids all have computer brains," you explain. "All we have to do is to give them a problem that they can't solve."

"But there are thousands of them," replies Psili. "We can't hop round giving them all problems."

You think hard for a moment. "I've got it," you cry. "Do you have powerful speaker systems here on Gargul?"

Psili thinks for a moment, "Yes, we've got huge speakers in the Wobbleball Stadium."

A quick journey to the Wobbleball Stadium and you have all the equipment you need – microphones, amplifiers, vast loudspeakers and all the wires.

Turn to **24**.

9

Arriving in the zone, you and Psili quickly assemble the equipment and line up the banks of powerful speakers.

"I just hope we're in the right place," says Psili, gazing up into the empty sky . . .

Turn to **213**.

10

One moment your atoms are streaking through space on a transporter beam and the next they've arranged themselves back into the shape of a boy.

You're back at home sitting in your living room. Homework books are spread out on the table in front of you.

Just as you're trying to gather your thoughts together, your mother walks into the room, pushing a vacuum cleaner. "Where did you sneak off to, my lad," she says. "I looked in here a moment ago and you weren't doing your homework. If it's not done by the time I've finished hoovering, you're in trouble."

You look at the books in front of you and see that the work isn't even started. While her back is turned you slip the transmuter from your pocket, enter the code, point it at your books, and press the button. WHOOSH. Three hours' homework done in a fraction of a second.

Your mother turns and picks up one of the books. "Well done, I see you're all finished," she says with a smile, "and I do believe that your handwriting is improving at last," she adds, pulling a bar of chocolate from her apron pocket.

Turn to **208**.

11

"It's from Psili," you cry with delight. "He's escaped from Ferrous and is heading back to Gargul. He's given us his position and says that if we can work out the coordinates, he'll teleport me back to his ship."

"Well, that'll save you a lot of time," agrees Twerp. "C'mon, jump into the teleporter and we'll give it a try."

You climb into the teleport capsule while Twerp sits at the controls.

"Now, if I can just figure out this last coordinate ..." he mumbles to himself. "OK, we're ready to roll. Adios, Earthkid." And with that he activates the teleport beam.

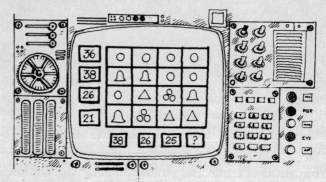

Find the missing number.

If you can work out the coordinate, turn to it.
If not, turn to **109**.

12

After a desperate search, you eventually think that you've found the damaged circuit. A few moments' work and it is repaired.

Turn to **5**.

13

Without a moment to spare, you connect the wires just as the first droid ship is landing.

The hatch bursts open and a horde of evil droids pour out towards you. Raising the microphone to your lips you speak the only words that can save the galaxy ...

But nothing comes out of the speakers. The leading droid raises a photon blaster, its eyes glowing red and evil.

A moment later you and Psili are lying motionless amongst the tangle of wires . . .

Well, Earthbrain, this is the end. You may have failed this time, but you can always try again. Who knows what strange beings you might meet on your next adventure . . .

14

"No, I'm sure we're in the right place," says Psili, not really looking very sure at all.

He looks around. The entire area is a tangle of wires. "Anyway, it would take us ages to sort this lot out again," he adds.

Suddenly, there's a noise behind you. Spinning round, a horrifying sight meets your eyes.

Turn to **217**.

15

You decide that there's just not enough time to go back and check so you'll have to stay where you are.

"If we are facing in the wrong direction, couldn't we turn some of the speakers to face the other way," suggests Psili.

"I don't think that there'd be enough power if we did," you reply. "If you really think that we're facing the wrong way, we should turn all the speakers round right now, before it's too late."

If you want to turn the speakers round, turn to **212**.
If not, turn to **14**.

16

Without a moment to spare, you connect the wires just as the first droid warship is landing.

The hatch bursts open and a horde of evil Ferrousian droids pour out towards you, brandishing laser cannons and photon blasters.

Raising the microphone to your lips, you take a deep breath and speak the only words that can save the galaxy . . .

"Which came first, the chicken or the egg?"

Your amplified voice booms through the powerful speakers at the approaching army of droids . . .

Turn to **218**.

17

You're beginning to get the hang of space travel and starting to feel a little more relaxed with this lumpy, yellow creature with all the fingers and eyes. The questions have been quite easy so far, you think to yourself, as you feel something brush against your leg.

Looking down, you see a small creature, rather

like a cross between a hamster and an elephant, a sort of hamster with a trunk.

"What's this?" you ask Psili.

"Oh, that's our cleaner. It's called a Twit. They keep our ships clean. We get them from Alto-Mimos. Due to their flexible trunks and their natural diet of dust, they make splendid cleaners."

You stroke the furry little cleaner which emits a sound like a cat being shaved.

"I don't think you're a Twit," you say. "I shall call you Hoover."

"Now we're on course for Gargul, shall we begin the data collection?" suggests Psili.

"All right, I'm ready," you reply, as Hoover curls up comfortably on your lap, sucking up the remains of the green froth from your school trousers.

"How long is a piece of string?" asks Psili suddenly, looking rather pleased with himself.

If it's five times 20% of its length, turn to **4**.
If it's twice as long as half of it, turn to **67**.
If it's about twenty-three centimetres, turn to **129**.

18

He leads you into a control room and up to a strange-looking machine. Sliding a small disc into a slot, Komyk tells you to pull the large gleaming lever. The machine bursts into life, lights flash, buzzers sound and everyone in the room begins to shout at once, "Nudge, pause, tilt, go for the bonus," and other, totally meaningless things.

Suddenly there's a loud grinding and clattering. "He's got the jackpot," they all cry, and thousands upon thousands of discs cascade onto the floor around your feet.

"Well, you must have done this before," says Komyk, with a wink. "Now you've passed the final test, I can tell you that we received a message from your friend, Commander Psili the Gargoid, some time ago. He told us that he had escaped from Ferrous and was looking for you."

"But where is he?" you plead.

"Don't worry, Earthling, we'll get you there," says Komyk. "All you have to do is step into the teleport cubicle."

You bid your new friends a hasty goodbye and step into the small chamber. You're weighed down by the huge sack of discs which Komyk has told you to keep.

Moments later you start to tingle and you know that you're on your way.

Turn to **35**.

19

You stamp along the corridor until you reach a doorway leading outside.

"How can they just give up, without even trying," you think angrily, as you activate the door panel.

The panel opens to reveal the gardens of the Imperial Palace. In the warm, humid atmosphere of Gargul, the plants are fantastic. There are huge blooms measuring several metres across and vast, towering palm-like trees crowd in profusion.

As you wander around, you begin to calm down. "If only I could think of some way to fight the droids," you are thinking as your attention is taken by a huge plant. It's covered in spiralling red tendrils. Unlike the other plants, it has a low fence around it.

"Wow, just think what that would look like in our back garden at home," you think to yourself. "Wouldn't Dad be surprised." Then you notice that there are several huge seed pods hanging from its tendrils, each split open showing clusters of blood-red seeds inside.

You're just about to clamber over the fence when you notice a sign attached to a stake in the ground nearby.

Ke Epwel
Lba Ckda
Nge Rou Sc
Arn Ivoro
Usp LanT

If you want to get some seeds, turn to **33**.

If you don't, turn to **228**.

20

You tap in the code and wait breathlessly.

"Identification received, you are cleared to land, prepare to lock on to homing beacon."

You look down on the planet Gargul. The lights of the Spaceport are twinkling far below. Gently the ship settles onto the landing pad, the hatch opens and there is Psili.

Rushing out, you are lifted from the ground by the happy Gargoid.

"Earthbrain, I thought I'd never see you again," he warbles joyfully.

You introduce Wire Twerp, who's eager to get back to Vas Legas and his prospecting, just in case there are any claim-jumpers about.

"So long, amigo," you shout, as you wave goodbye to the space cowboy and his departing ship.

Psili hurries you along. "We must go to my leader and tell him of RU12's evil plans so that we can prepare ourselves."

Turn to **71**.

21

Your hand closes on the lever to the left. You pull it hard. The ship begins to turn slowly away from the vast gaping jaws. As you breathe a sigh of relief, the view through the screen starts to spin. The ship is spiralling towards a whirling mass of spinning gas.

"Xpiqs rrhiphs!" exclaims Psili, "we're losing thrust and heading towards a black hole. Quick, push the thrust control up to maximum!"

As you turn to the controls, the ship lurches. Psili is catapulted across the cabin and lands heavily. "Which control?" you scream, but he's been knocked out.

Which of the controls is the thrust?

*If it's A, turn to **2**.*
*If it's B, turn to **41**.*
*If it's C, turn to **220**.*

22

Without a moment to spare, you connect the wires just as the first droid ship is landing. The hatch bursts open and a horde of evil droids pour out towards you.

Raising the microphone to your lips, you speak the only words that can save the galaxy . . .

But nothing comes out of the speakers, not a sound. You can't have taken enough care mending the broken circuit board. The leading droid raises a photon blaster, its eyes glowing red and evil.

A moment later you and Psili are lying motionless amongst the tangle of wires . . .

Well, Earthbrain, this is the end. You may have failed this time, but you can always try again. Who knows what strange beings you might meet on your next adventure . . .

23

When the electrodes are fitted, RU12 turns to the control console. As his back is turned, you search your pockets for some kind of weapon. Suddenly you find a small tube of superglue. Unscrewing the top, you await your chance and as he takes a step closer you reach forward, squirting the contents around the droid's feet.

A moment later he turns, that is, his body turns but his feet stay just where they were.

Tearing the electrodes from your head, you leap up and race for the door. RU12 tries to grab you as you rush past, but he leans a bit too far. You reach the passageway to the sound of a resounding crash, glancing back to see that RU12 and his feet seem to have parted company.

Running along the dimly-lit corridor you hear a familiar warble, and head for the sound.

Go to **100**.

24

Assembling the mass of equipment, you switch on to test it.

Nothing happens, it's completely dead. You check the speakers and microphone which are all fine.

"It must be the amplifier. There's probably a broken connection," you explain to the Gargoid, as you remove the casing to expose a mass of wires and circuit boards, "and we've got to find it quickly."

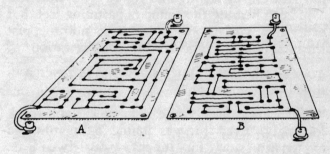

If circuit A has a broken connection, turn to **12**.
If circuit B has a broken connection, turn to **193**.

25

Psili tries desperately to swing the ship away from the rapidly-approaching laser bolt, but it's no good. The weapon's guidance device is locked on to the heat of your ship's exhaust gases.

"Sorry about this, Earthbrain," says Psili, as the ship explodes in a ball of white-hot gas.

Well, Earthbrain, this is the end. You may have failed this time, but you can always try again. Who knows what strange beings you might meet on your next adventure . . .

26

You decide to head for the mountain. From up there you may be able to see if there are any other signs of intelligent life on this planet.

Struggling through the dense undergrowth you have the creepy feeling that you're being watched. You keep hearing the sound of pattering feet, but every time you turn to look, there's nothing, just the buzz of insects and the dripping vegetation.

Your clothes are in tatters and you're covered in mud from the swamp.

"I wish I was back home right now," you think longingly, "even if it was double maths followed by gristle stew for lunch" (your two least favourite things).

Suddenly, something moves amongst the leaves. You crouch and freeze . . .

Turn to 7.

27

You run and run until the corridor comes to an end. There's a small compartment with an open

hatch. On the wall inside is some sort of map which must show the various levels inside the planet Ferrous.

A control panel with just two buttons is on the wall beside it. One button has an arrow pointing up and the other has an arrow pointing down.

If you want to go up, turn to **222**.
If you want to go down, turn to **192**.

28

You swing majestically over the raging river, but about halfway across the creeper comes away in your hands and you plummet onto the jagged rocks below. "AAAaaRRRaaAAA," you cry, but this time it's not a Tarzan impression.

Well, Earthbrain, this is the end. You may have failed this time, but you can always try again. Who knows what strange beings you might meet on your next adventure . . .

29

"That's most odd, Earthbrain. Our own measurements indicate a circumference of 24,902 miles," queries a puzzled Psili.

"Ah, that's because you haven't allowed for the fact that the Earth is slightly flattened at the poles," you reply smugly. "The figure I gave you is for the meridional circumference."

Turn to **34**.

30

Soon you're on the way to Gargul, safely aboard Wire Twerp's ship.

"How long will it take us to get there?" you ask.

"Oh, we'll be there quicker'n a possum up a tree."

"But how long's that?" you snap, getting rather tired of all the western talk.

"'bout two, three weeks," he replies.

"*What*?" you yell. "Two or three weeks? It could be too late by then."

At that moment the cowboy holds up a hand to

silence you. "Hush there, we've got a message comin' in. I'll put it up on the screen." The message appears but is so scrambled Twerp tells you that there must be some interference.

If you can read the message, turn to the number indicated.
If you can't, turn to 53.

31

As you crawl further into the ventilation shaft, it seems to be getting darker. Very soon it's become so dark that you can't see a thing.

If you have a torch, turn to 64.
If not, turn to 6.

32

Your body tingles as the teleporter is activated . . .

Turn to 35.

33

"I wish I could read this stupid Gargoid language," you think, "but it's probably only the plant's name." A quick heave and you're over the fence and reaching for the nearest seed pod.

Just as your hand closes over it, there's a rustling sound and a red tendril snakes towards you like lightning. "Argh!" you scream, as the tendril winds itself tightly around your waist. More tendrils grip you and you're lifted from the ground. Looking down, you see that a huge bloom is opening below you like a gigantic mouth.

You scream and shout, but there's nobody else in the garden. You feel yourself slipping inside the huge flower. Then there's only darkness as it closes – with you inside.

Well, Earthbrain, this is the end. You may have failed this time, but you can always try again. Who knows what strange beings you might meet on your next adventure . . .

34

The Gargoid spacecraft does a quick circumnavigation of the Earth (all 24,902 miles of it, having taken the equatorial route), before hurtling off into black, star-spangled space.

You're shown to your own hammock and offered a dish of green froth. Unfortunately, being unused to eating green froth whilst sitting in a hammock, you spill most of it on your school trousers.

"Oh no," you think, "I'll be in trouble now." Then, with a smile, you imagine how you can be in trouble with a frog.

"Tell me, Earthbrain," asks Psili suddenly, "to which group of Earth life-forms does man belong?"

If man is a primate, turn to **17**.
If man is an crustacean, turn to **44**.
If man is a plant, turn to **129**.

35

Millions of miles are telescoped into seconds as the atoms of your body are beamed through space. Suddenly you feel yourself getting together again, and there's Psili, hopping around excitedly.

"Earthbrain, I thought we'd never see you again," he says, wrapping his long yellow arms around you and lifting you off the ground.

Turn to **60**.

36

Continuing straight ahead, you eventually see stripes of light on the shaft wall. Crawling closer you find that it's a grille through which you can see a brightly-lit corridor. Just beyond the grille, the tunnel comes to an end. So, unless you can escape through the grille, you'll just have to go back the way you came.

Grasping the grille you pull and pull, but it's securely fixed in place. You're tired, hungry, your knees are sore and bleeding and you've just about had enough.

You brush against the grille as you turn to go back along the narrow shaft and to your surprise and relief it swings slowly outwards on its hinges.

A quick scramble through the small opening and you're outside in the corridor.

To go left, turn to **81**.
To go right, turn to **27**.

37

You can see six faces peering at you through the undergrowth. Leaping up you sprint off, just as a tiny dart flashes past you and embeds itself in a tree.

Running as fast as you can, you hear the patter of feet behind you, but gradually they fade into the distance.

Looking ahead you can see that the lofty snow-covered mountain is getting closer.

Turn to **62**.

38

You connect the wires, and the control panel instantly comes to life, lights flashing and the screen showing 'ALL SYSTEMS OPERATIVE'.

You pull a lever marked 'DISENGAGE', and the pod separates from Psili's ship. With thrust set to maximum and the control stick wrenched over, the tiny escape pod rockets away.

The huge steel jaws are just closing as the pod darts through the opening and out into the blackness of space.

Looking through the screen you see Psili's ship

engulfed by the vast mechanical monster. You wonder if you'll ever see him again . . .

Turn to **61**.

39

"Absolutely correct, didn't he do well?" yells Komyk, slapping you on the back. "And now for tonight's star prize (your life), can you tell us what 'Stephenson's Rocket' was?"

If you think it was a firework, turn to **130**.
If you think it was a railway engine, turn to **157**.

40

After a few seconds of desperate thought you manage to work out the code and enter it into the communication computer. As soon as the code is entered you hear the voice again.

"Identification code received, you are cleared to land."

Psili looks relieved. "Well done, Earthbrain, you've saved our mission once again."

Turn to **123**.

41

You feel the thrust increasing. The spinning gradually begins to slow down as the ship's powerful engines fight against the dreadful pull of the black hole.

On hearing a groan behind you, you turn to see

Psili staggering to his foot, looking more wobbly than usual. He hops to the screen. "Well done," he says, seeing the black hole fade away in the distance. "Now let's get home to Gargul."

Turn to **119**.

42

Feeling a lot better after something to eat, you start wondering what to do next. You don't have to wonder for very long as the screen in front of you bursts into life.

"It must be some kind of message," you think, trying to understand the strange symbols on the glowing display. Suddenly you notice that a ship is approaching your tiny craft. It's too far away to make out what type of ship it is, but you're pretty sure that the message must be coming from it.

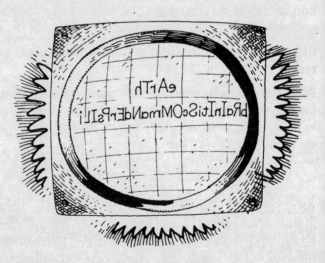

"It could be someone coming to help me," you think. "But on the other hand, it could be someone coming to blow me into tiny pieces."

If you want to wait and see, turn to **58**.
If you want to escape, turn to **118**.

43

It's no good, you can't see anything, so you decide to continue with your journey. Just as you stand up, you feel a slight prick in your arm. Looking down you see a tiny dart sticking in your flesh. It's only about three inches long with a small red feather flight.

Your mouth suddenly feels very dry. You try to lift your hand to wipe it, but somehow your arm just won't move. Everything starts to get misty and blurred.

Falling to the ground, you're aware of being surrounded by tiny jabbering faces, but it doesn't . . . really . . . seem . . . to . . . matter . . .

Well, Earthbrain, this is the end. You may have failed this time, but you can always try again. Who knows what strange beings you might meet on your next adventure . . .

44

Psili looks disappointed. "I asked you this question not because we didn't know the answer, but to test if we had located the right Earthling," he says. "Obviously our transporter coordinates were incorrect," he adds, whilst reaching for a bright red lever. You feel your body begin to dissolve.

"Oh no," you think, "not the transporter beam, not again . . ."

Turn to **80**.

45

"Excellent, the Gargoids were right, your brain is a very fine organism."

"Thank you very much," you say, feeling rather pleased with yourself until you remember why he's interested in it.

"However," he growls, "if you fail the tests, I will pull this lever and the result won't be very pleasant for you, Earthling."

With this threat still ringing in your ears the screen displays another mind-boggling puzzle.

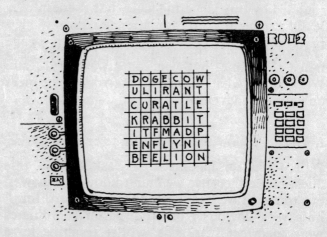

How many animals can you find on this grid, looking horizontally, vertically and diagonally?

A 11
B 12

*If you think the answer is A, turn to **182**.*
*If you think the answer is B, turn to **75**.*

46

Hauling yourself up the steep rock on the rope is much easier than climbing. You can see the jungle spread far beneath you like a green carpet and in the distance the glint of a winding river.

It comes as rather a nasty shock when the rope suddenly goes limp. Your fingers scrabble for a grip on the smooth rock as you begin to fall.

Down and down you plummet, thinking that you must be very high, because the people below look just like ants . . . Thud.

Well, Earthbrain, this is the end. You may have failed this time, but you can always try again. Who knows what strange beings you might meet on your next adventure . . .

47

It's no good, you just can't seem to break the code. You can only stay with Psili and see what fate awaits you.

*Turn to **180**.*

The pods stop, and you, Psili and Hoover climb out on to the platform. There are several important-looking Gargoids waiting for you. They're dressed in lavish uniforms with gold braid and brightly- coloured sashes.

"It's the Imperial Gargle Guard," whispers Psili. You both follow the guards into a lift which streaks upwards like a rocket. Looking out through the plastic walls you can see the city of Gargoplex stretching out below you in all directions.

The lift comes to a rather sudden stop. Unfortunately your stomach doesn't stop with it and continues up to hit your chin before returning to its normal position.

You are led into a magnificent chamber, where at the far end sits an impressive figure. A uniformed guard steps forward.

"Pray be silent for the Lord High Gargler, Protector of all Gargoids, Emperor of the Gargonian System, Phyck the Ninety-Forth."

At this point, both you and Psili bow low until your heads almost touch the ground. A voice rings out, "You may rise and come forward." At this command you and Psili approach the Lord High Gargler himself.

Psili tells of your adventures and of RU12's plans to destroy all life and rule the galaxy. Phyck looks at you both, his face a troubled frown, "We must call a Battle Council straight away."

After a rest and some welcome but rather odd food, you are both called before the Battle Council.

Entering a long chamber you're seated at a vast table with splendidly-dressed Gargoids sitting all around it.

Phyck addresses the council, "Members of the Imperial Battle Council, you are all now aware of the threat we face from RU12 and his army of androids," he begins. "Commander Psili and this noble Earthling have endured great perils to warn us of the evil droid's plot. We must now decide how we can best defend our planet."

After endless discussion, it's clear that the Gargoids haven't a chance against the heavily-armed droids. "Perhaps if we surrender they may spare us," says Phyck sadly.

At this you leap to your feet and storm out of the chamber. "Well, you can surrender if you like, but I'm certainly not going to give up that easily."

But what can one small Earthling do against an army of powerful androids?

If you want to go to your quarters, turn to **8**.
If you want to go outside, turn to **19**.

49

"Well, I'll be darned if you're not plum right," said Twerp, slipping the two pearl-handled Colts back into their holsters. "You must be from Earth, all right, but how in tarnation did you end up here?"

You tell him the long story of your adventures and how you need to find Psili to warn him of RU12's plans.

"Well, pardner, let's hit the trail pronto," he says, removing the saddle from the caterpillar and sending it off with a slap on the rump. "Adios, amigo," he calls, as the beast lollops away.

Turn to **30**.

50

As you enter the code the huge steel hatch beside the guard droid opens with a hiss . . .

Turn to **98**.

51

You press on through the dark and menacing jungle. Every sound sets your heart pounding. You're too frightened to stop and rest until the first rays of dawn penetrate the gloomy forest.

As the twin suns rise, you realize that you are completely lost. Climbing a tree you see a lofty mountain in the distance, shrouded in mist, and nearby you hear the sounds of rushing water.

If you want to go towards the mountain, turn to **26**.
If you want to go towards the water, turn to **85**.

52

There's only one good thing to be said about travelling by transporter beam, it's quick. Apart from that it's about as much fun as having your teeth extracted whilst sitting a maths exam.

As soon as the atoms of your brain get themselves together enough to think, "Where am I?" your eyes have appeared and, luckily for you, there's one on each side of your nose.

They open, look around and then close again with shock. Eventually you realize that you can't stand there all day with your eyes closed, so you try again.

There before you stands the strangest and most repulsive creature you've ever seen, with the possible exception of Mr Hardgraft, your maths teacher.

"Welcome, Earthbrain," warbles the creature, with a friendly smile. This presents you with two problems. The first is that you haven't got a clue what he's saying, and the second is that you're not sure that it's a smile or even a mouth doing it.

You stand there looking blank (not a very difficult undertaking) as, with a gleam in several eyes, the creature suddenly offers you what looks like a pair of large, rubber joke ears.

Not wishing to spoil his fun, you put on the stereo trans-lugs, feeling almost as stupid as you look.

The next time the creature warbles, the sounds become words. "Welcome, Earthbrain, I am Psili," he repeats. "Our sensors have indicated that you are the most intelligent organism of your species."

With a flush of pride you think, "so that's why nobody seems to understand me."

"My mission," continues the creature, "is to collect data concerning your planet and we feel that you are the best-equipped to assist us in this quest."

After a moment of thought you speak your first words to this alien being, the first words he has ever heard an Earthman utter, "What's it worth then?"

With another smile, or something, the creature replies. "We have the technology to make almost any wish come true."

"Could you turn someone into a frog?" you ask hopefully, starting to list some suitable candidates.

"We can transform organic matter, if you wish it," he replies. "However, in return you must supply me with accurate data."

Although you're not really sure what data is, you agree readily. "It's a deal. What data do you want me to give you first?"

"Before we begin," warns the alien, "if the data you give us is not correct, we will transport you back to Earth, and you shall receive no rewards.

"Let me set a course for our planet," the creature says, as he settles his rippling bulk into a sort of hammock, "but before we leave your Earth, perhaps you'll tell me its circumference, for our records."

If it's about 24,860 miles, turn to **29**.
If it's about 24,902 miles, turn to **34**.
If it's about 125 miles, turn to **129**.

53

After what seems like an endless journey, Twerp tells you that you're approaching the planet Gargul.

As the planet comes into sight, a message is received over the communication system.

"This is Gargul Defence Control, please give the identification code. If it is not received within thirty seks, the auto-defence system will be activated."

A grid appears on the screen. "I'm sure I can remember this from Psili's ship," you say hopefully, as you begin to enter the code at the communication keyboard.

Find the identity code and go to it.

Clues Down

1. A cloth house
2. Keeps birds warm
3. A roof covering
4. To let someone borrow
5. A stinging plant
6. Dried grass

If you can work out the code, turn to the number indicated.

*If not, turn to **88**.*

54

At the last moment you understand the sign and pull the control lever over to the left. The pod screams around the curve just in time.

Turn to **102**.

55

"What do you think RU12 wants us for?" you ask Psili with a gulp.

"He must think we know something about his invasion plans, whatever they are," replies Psili.

After some hours, you hear sounds in the corridor outside. The bolts on the door slide and the door opens. The squat droid comes in carrying a tray. "Why Lord RU12 wants you kept in good condition, I don't know," he mumbles as he deposits the tray on the floor of the cell.

If you have a water pistol, turn to **138**.
If not, turn to **77**.

56

You feel yourself sliding down a shaft, slowly at first and then faster and faster. You're tumbling over and over, falling, falling . . .

Turn to **192**.

57

You choose course A and Psili prepares for the jump to light speed.

"Strap yourself in good and tight," he says, his finger poised over a large red button. "Here we go."

The engine speed increases and the whole ship is quivering. Psili looks like a lemon jelly on a spin-dryer as the stars change from points of light into multi-coloured streaks.

You notice a point of light in the centre of the screen getting bigger and bigger at an incredible speed.

"Look out," you scream, "we're going to hit a . . ." BOOM.

Well, Earthbrain, this is the end. You may have failed this time, but you can always try again. Who knows what strange beings you might meet on your next adventure . . .

58

Looking back at the screen you realize that the message is coming from Psili's ship, which is now rapidly approaching.

With a loud clang, the Gargoid ship docks with the tiny escape pod and you hear the hiss of the airlock opening.

Turn to 73.

59

You tell the lengthy story of your adventures so far, and how you were separated from Psili and the Gargoid ship.

The Vas Legasians listen intently and only giggle a bit at the most unpleasant parts.

"The machine you escaped from," explains Komyk, "was a Ferrousian salvage droid. The planet Ferrous is ruled by RU12, a monstrous android, who is planning to take over this galaxy and destroy all organic life. RU12 has spies throughout the galaxy. We must be sure that you are telling the truth. If you are really from Earth, as you claim, tell us what the Earthling Liam Brady is famous for?"

If you think he's a ballet dancer, turn to 130.
If you think he's a footballer, turn to 39.

60

Psili tells you of his adventures, how he escaped from Ferrous and that he must return to Gargul to warn his people of RU12's evil plans.

"You have returned just at the right time," says Psili. "We are approaching my planet now."

Turn to 122.

61

As the tiny escape pod leaves the salvage droid far behind, you begin to realize the situation you've got yourself into.

You're alone in a tiny spacecraft, you've no idea where you are and you don't even know how to drive the thing properly. What's even worse, you're beginning to feel rather hungry.

If you have some chocolate, turn to 221.
If not, turn to 97.

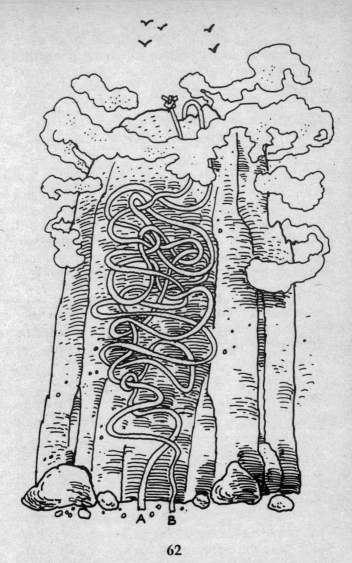

A   B

62

Reaching the base of the mountain, you begin to
climb. The rock is steep and slippery but you can
see some ropes hanging down, just above you.

"There's a bit of luck," you think to yourself. There are two ropes, both of which disappear into the mist above your head.

Which one should you use?

If you choose rope A, turn to **167**.
If you choose rope B, turn to **46**.

63

Taking the stub of chalk from your pocket, you make a mark on the wall. As you make your way along the tunnels you mark each turning and soon discover that you've been going round in circles.

Setting off again you find yourself at the entrance to a massive chamber with a high vaulted ceiling. Glancing around the huge room, you see at the far end a figure sitting on a block of carved stone.

You call, "Hello there, hooded figure," but there's no reply so you walk boldly, but perhaps rather stupidly, towards the figure whose head is completely covered by the hood of a long flowing cloak . . .

Turn to **110**.

64

Taking the torch from your pocket, you shine the beam ahead. It's the one that you use for reading under the covers in bed so it's lucky that the batteries aren't dead.

With horror you see that just in front of you is a gaping shaft into which you would have fallen. Edging around the hole you come to a junction. You can go left, right or straight ahead.

If you want to go left, turn to **56**.
If you want to go right, turn to **114**.
If you want to go straight ahead, turn to **36**.

65

As you walk along the corridor you see an open hatchway ahead. Pushing the droid off-balance you race towards the hatch.

Turn to **227**.

66

As you press the button marked A, there is a loud rumbling as the huge blast doors to the docking bay begin to slide shut.

You quickly find a place to hide behind a small shuttlecraft just as you hear the clatter of droids approaching. Peering out, you see that the guard droids are searching the docking bay.

"It's no good staying here or we're bound to be caught," you suggest to Psili. "Let's see if we can find a way to reach your ship without bumping into the guards."

Turn to **197**.

"That's most useful," says Psili, entering this valuable information into the data bank.

"Why did you want to know?" you enquire.

"Well," begins Psili, "we've been monitoring Earth broadcasts for some time and we heard this question asked in a political debate, yet with all our computer resources we were unable to answer it."

At that moment an alarm starts to wail. Psili leaps to his foot. "Quick, action stations, we're being attacked."

On the screen you see a vast shape approaching rapidly, its front end opening up like a huge gaping mouth.

Psili, hopping to the controls, trips over Hoover and falls in a wobbly, yellow heap.

"Hurry," he cries, "pull the starboard control lever, quickly." You rush to the controls. There are three gleaming levers, one on the left, one on the right and one in the middle. But which one should you pull?

If you want to pull the left lever, turn to **21**.
If you want to pull the right lever, turn to **163**.
If you want to pull the middle lever, turn to **90**.

As you hear the sounds of the Black Slobbering Guzzlecruncher beginning to recover, the door suddenly swings open. You leap out, slamming it behind you, and race off down the corridor.

You're just slowing down to decide which way to go, when you hear a familiar warble and run towards the source of the sound.

Turn to **100**.

69

You do your best but you can't understand the message at all. Through the view screen you can see that the ship is passing through a belt of huge rugged asteroids.

There's a sudden cry from Psili. "The sensors have indicated that a large force of warships is in our immediate area. We must change course quickly."

Psili grabs the controls but, just as the ship starts to turn, there's a flash of light as something passes at high speed. "Look, we're surrounded," screams Psili, pointing out through the view screen.

From behind every asteroid a Ferrousian warship has appeared and bolts of photon torpedoes are narrowly missing your ship.

"Engage shields," orders Psili, but it's too late. The next torpedo hits the main fuel tank and your ship is atomized in a white-hot fireball . . .

Well, Earthbrain, this is the end. You may have failed this time, but you can always try again. Who knows what strange beings you might meet on your next adventure . . .

You are taken into a large chamber where every wall has banks of controls and flashing displays. RU12 drops you onto a padded couch, above which hangs a glass dome festooned with wires and switches.

"As you may be donating your brain in a worth-while cause," begins the android, "I will explain why I have need of it. I have long known the limitations of computer technology and have there-fore perfected the use of an electro-organic brain. However, until recently the Androxian Megapod was thought to be the galaxy's most intelligent organic life-form." He leaned closer, "That is, until I intercepted a transmission from a Gargoid ship. This transmission told me that the Gargoids had located a life-form with capabilities far in excess of the Megapod. We must now test these capabilities." With that, he spins the couch to face a large screen.

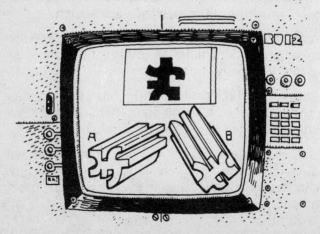

Which key will fit the lock?

*If you think the answer is A, turn to **45**.*
*If you think the answer is B, turn to **103**.*

71

"Follow me," says Psili, "we'll go in a hoverpod. The terminal is just around here. By the way, I've brought a friend of yours along."

He reaches into one of his pouches and pulls out Hoover, the furry little cleaner from the ship. The creature squeals with delight and leaps into your arms, snuffling in your ear with its trunk-like nose.

"Here we are," calls Psili, climbing into a tiny carriage like the ones on a big dipper. "You get into the one behind. Don't worry, they've got magnetic couplings, you won't get lost." So you scramble in, settling Hoover down on your lap.

There's a sudden lurch and off you go shooting at high speed down a transparent tube.

*Turn to **187**.*

72

Peering through the trees you can see four small faces watching you.

Leaping to your feet you are about to run when a

net drops over you from the branches above. You thrash around and struggle, but it's no good, you're trapped.

Turn to **136**.

73

The hatch slides open and in hops Psili. He bounds across the cabin like a runaway pogo stick and sweeps you into the air.

"I'm so pleased I've found you," he warbles excitedly. "Had you not activated the distress beacon I could never have located you."

"What distress beacon?" you reply. Psili gestures to the little red light still blinking on and off.

"Now, there's no time to waste. I must tell you the awful news," begins Psili. "We were captured and taken to the planet Ferrous where the evil android RU12 is building a huge army of robots. His aim is to destroy all organic life in the galaxy so that it can be ruled by androids. We were lucky to escape and now we must return to Gargul and warn my leaders of this threat."

Turn to **84**.

74

In the dim light you can just see the compass needle as you crawl along the shafts. By keeping in the same direction you should be able to avoid going round and round in circles.

After a while you come to a junction. You could go left or right, but a look at the compass tells you to keep going straight ahead.

Turn to **36**.

"You've just escaped a very unpleasant death," he says, looking almost disappointed. "Let us continue with the test." With that, an even more difficult puzzle appears on the screen.

How many times does RU12's name appear on this grid?

A = 16 times
B = 14 times

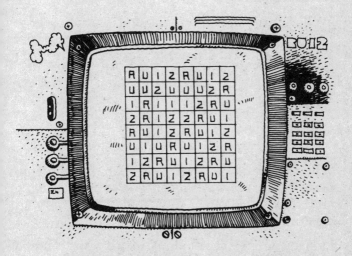

If you think the answer is A, turn to **1**.
If you think the answer is B, turn to **182**.

76

Taking a deep breath you press the button marked B. There's a motor sound, followed by a hiss that grows louder, louder and LOUDER. Spinning round in the pilot's chair, you see with horror that the hatch is beginning to open . . .

You press the button again and again but it's no good, it won't shut. The air is rushing out of the cabin and the pull is getting stronger. You can't hold on much longer. Gradually your fingers are torn from the arms of the chair and you are sucked through the hatch into space.

Spinning over and over you can't hold your breath much longer . . .

Well, Earthbrain, this is the end. You may have failed this time, but you can always try again. Who knows what strange beings you might meet on your next adventure . . .

77

When the guard has left, you examine the contents of the tray. Although you're very hungry, one look is enough to completely ruin your appetite.

Lying there in a sea of slimy-looking green liquid are several large whitish grubs.

"Yuk! what's that?" you ask Psili, whilst trying to control your queasy stomach.

"They're Phaal Larva, and a real delicacy too," replies Psili, settling down on the floor by the tray, "and if I'm not mistaken they're stuffed with fuggleberries and sour murch."

As Psili tucks in, you have to retire to the far end of the cell until he's finished slurping. Settling back and gently patting his wobbly stomach, Psili looks quite content. "If RU12 is feeding us with treats like this," he says, "we've obviously nothing much to worry about."

As you are wondering why the android would want to treat his prisoners so well, the cell door opens. In comes the guard droid.

"You, Earthling, Lord RU12 is ready for you now. I hope you enjoyed the meal, it's likely to be your last one." With a chuckle, rather like a car trying to start on a cold morning, the droid drags you protesting out into the corridor.

After being hauled none too gently along the corridors by the droid, you reach a large steel doorway with a guard on either side. Some kind of password is given and the doors slide open.

Turn to **98**.

Turn to **98**.

78

You set off boldly through the swamp, brushing the swarms of insects away from your face. Although the ground is squelchy, it is fairly solid under your feet.

Deeper and deeper into the jungle you go, pushing aside the branches and hanging creepers and trying to remember the route. Eventually you reach a clearing with several paths leading from it.

"Was it left here or straight across and then left," you ponder. "Oh well, I'll try left."

Halfway across the clearing your feet start to sink and as you desperately struggle to pull one foot out, the other just sinks in deeper.

You're up to your waist now, grabbing at the plants to pull yourself out, but they just come out in your hands.

You're slowly sinking deeper and deeper, shoulders . . . neck . . . chin . . . AAARRRGGGHHH!!

Well, Earthbrain, this is the end. You may have failed this time, but you can always try again. Who knows what strange beings you might meet on your next adventure . . .

79

As you are trying to think what to do next, a red light begins to flash and a warning bleeper starts to bleep. "That means the shields are weakening. In a few moments, the droids' blasters will break through and then we've had it," warns Psili. You look at the hole again – is it worth taking a chance?

If you think it is, turn to **145**.
If you don't, turn to **113**.

80

You find yourself back on good old Earth, seated uncomfortably in the dentist's chair.

He's coming at you with great steel pincers which suddenly remind you that crustaceans are crabs.

Oh dear, too late.

Well, Earthbrain, this is the end. You may have failed this time, but you can always try again. Who knows what strange beings you might meet on your next adventure . . .

81

You run off to the left along the corridor. Turning a corner you find yourself face to face with a huge, gleaming android.

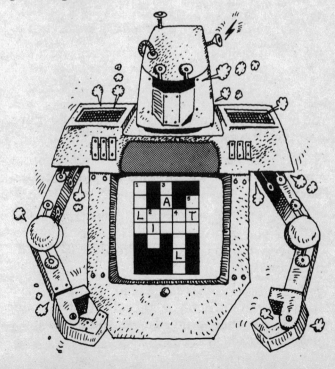

"Enter your identity code," grates the menacing droid, gripping your shoulder, none too gently, with one vast steel fist.

On its chest is a screen with something like a keyboard below it. Displayed on the screen are rows of boxes and some strange phrases. The grip on your shoulder begins to tighten . . .

Find the code number.

Clues Down

1. A pack member
2. If it's very quiet, you can hear one drop
3. What you get if you

divide into two equal parts.
4. Not moving
5. Fit for a pig

If you can discover your identity code, turn to it.
If you can't, turn to **112**.

82

You pull the cable which just falls to the floor in a loose coil. It wasn't connected to anything.

At that moment you feel a strange sensation in your head and the room begins to spin faster and faster.

You have a feeling that your brain is being sucked out. But you don't think that for very long, because you haven't got anything left to do the thinking with.

Well, Earthbrain, this is the end. You may have failed this time, but you can always try again. Who knows what strange beings you might meet on your next adventure . . .

With a flash of inspiration (that even your maths teacher would have been proud of), you key in the number.

With a quick tug the clamp slips off the wheel.

"Quick," says Psili, "I can hear the droids coming back." You both race up the ramp into the ship, Psili closes the hatch and wobbles into the pilot's couch. At that moment you see the droids begin to open fire on the ship. Activating the shields, Psili turns to you. "The shields will hold them off for a while, but we'd better get out of here . . ." His voice fades and his cluster of eyes open wide. "Oh no," he gasps, "I've just thought of something . . ."

Turn to **161**.

"We must now prepare for a jump to light speed so that we reach Gargul in time to warn them of the invasion," explained Psili. "Our naviputer isn't working so we'll have to plot a course on the star map."

With that, he unrolls a huge map showing the locations of all the stars and planets in the system.

Psili points at the map, "There's our current location and there's the Planet Gargul. We must take great care that our course avoids the gravitational pull of the planets."

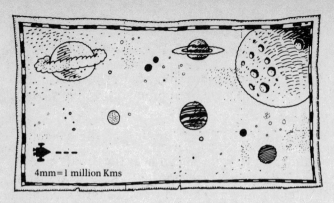

4mm = 1 million Kms

Which course will enable you to reach Gargul safely?

Course A	Course B
3 million kms	2.5 million kms
90° starboard	90° port
.5 million kms	4 million kms
90° port	90° starboard
5 million kms	3 million kms
90° port	90° starboard
3 million kms	.5 million kms
90° starboard	90° port
7.5 million kms	9.5 million kms
90° port	
1 million kms	

If you choose course A, turn to **57**.
If you choose course B, turn to **99**.

85

You fight your way through the undergrowth towards the sound of rushing water. After a little while you find yourself on the edge of a steep rocky gorge. Far below is a swiftly-running river.

Looking across the river you can see a strange-looking vehicle on the far bank. It has caterpillar tracks like a tank and huge wings folded along its back.

Turn to **214**.

86

Arriving at the creatures' encampment, you're deposited into a large pot hanging over a roaring fire. A rather fat little creature with a strange hat on is humming cheerfully to himself whilst sprinkling herbs over your head.

"Wait," you shout. "I'm not properly ripe yet. I'll be much tastier if you let me grow up a bit first," you add hopefully. But the creatures don't take any notice, they're far too busy peeling vegetables and laying the table.

You try and think what James Bond would do if he was in the pot, but your wristwatch doesn't turn into a flame-thrower and you haven't got a mini helicopter hidden in the heel of your shoe, so you give up.

The water's getting a bit hot now and you think you're starting to hear things as there's a buzzing noise in your head. The noise gets louder and the little creatures start to look up nervously. The buzzing turns into a whistling roar and the creatures scatter, shrieking in terror.

"Oh no," you think to yourself, "out of the cooking pot and into the . . ."

Turn to **95**.

Your ship is just a tiny speck in the vastness of space. Although you're still relieved to have escaped from the droid, you're not really so sure what to do next.

Suddenly the ship lurches, you grab the controls but it seems to have no effect. The controls are all dead but the ship is moving backwards, pulled by some unknown force.

Through the tiny rear view screen you can see the vast bulk of another ship close behind.

There's a loud clang as it docks with the tiny pod. A whirring of motors warns you that the airlock is about to open.

Stepping back in terror you prepare to defend yourself . . .

Turn to **73**.

"It's no good," you admit, "I just can't remember the code." Twerp calls you to the view screen.

"Looks like we've got visitors," he says, pointing to the slim, deadly missiles heading towards the ship.

"Can't we shoot them down?" you ask.

"This is just a prospecting ship, it's not armed. I've just got these," says Twerp, drawing his sixguns, "but they won't get me without a fight."

Quickly donning a space suit, Twerp is out of the

airlock before you can stop him. "This looks like the last shoot out. Adios, amigo," he calls, as the hatch closes.

The last thing you see is Wire Twerp with sixguns blazing as he faces the oncoming missiles . . .

Well, Earthbrain, this is the end. You may have failed this time, but you can always try again. Who knows what strange beings you might meet on your next adventure . . .

89

As you search in vain, the creature lunges. Luckily for you its huge size gives you an advantage.

You dart between its legs and run towards the door where you can see an illuminated panel.

Turn to **126**.

90

You pull on the middle lever, despite a groan from Psili. "You Vantralian waffle-head," he screams, "surely you know that starboard is right."

Your gaze returns to the viewing screen which darkens as the ship passes between the huge steel jaws.

In a moment of sheer panic, you notice a small hatch beside you with a control panel marked ESCAPE POD. On impulse you rush to the controls and see a row of flashing numerals with a blank space at the end with the words "INPUT ACCESS CODE" above.

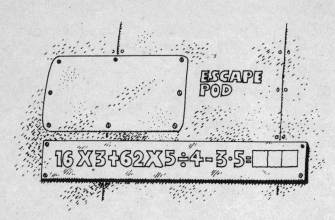

Find the missing number.

If you can break the code, turn to the number indicated.

If you can't break the code, turn to 47.

Player's Note: *If you arrive at a location and it doesn't tell you that you've successfully opened the escape pod hatch, you have got the answer wrong and must return to 90.*

91

The droid leads you along a dimly-lit corridor, its single optical sensor glowing in the middle of its dome-like head.

It has a wire leading to its aural receptor, connected to a small box on its belt and is humming happily to itself as it drags you along. You gesture to the box and the droid removes the plug from its 'ear'. There's a horrible grinding noise coming from it, like an engine that needs servicing.

"It's QT and the Solenoids," the droid informs you, tapping his Sopy Walkdroid. "My favourite track, 'I've got my modem working, baby'. Great, isn't it?" You nod in agreement, but are grateful when he replaces the plug.

As you continue along the corridor, you realize that the droid is more interested in his 'music' than he is in you. Suddenly you have an idea.

If you have some chewing gum, turn to **111**.
If you don't, turn to **65**.

92

If you twist slightly, you can just get your hand into your trouser pocket. A little more effort and the gleaming penknife is in your grasp.

The sharp blade cuts easily through the bonds and just as the monster is licking its lips you leap clear and race for the cover of the jungle.

Turn to **51**.

93

Entering the tiny escape pod, you slip into the pilot's couch. "If Psili is in grave danger, it's better if I can escape and get help," you think to yourself as you pull the lever marked DISENGAGE, and the pod drops away from the ship with a lurch.

The engines start and the pod is soon streaking away from the stricken Gargoid craft.

Away to your right you can see a planet swathed in mist. "Oh well, I've got to go somewhere. Maybe I'll find someone to help us," you think, as you swing the tiny craft towards the distant misty planet.

Turn to **173**.

94

"Just like I said," snarls Wire Twerp, "a filthy, thievin', lyin', cheatin', low-down claim-jumpin' skunk, if ever I saw one."

His hands flash to the sixguns hanging at his side in one blurred movement. BANG! BANG!

He blows the smoke from the barrels of his guns, spins them expertly round his fingers and slips them back into their holsters.

Looking down at your body lying in the dust, he sighs, "There's always someone faster on the draw, kid," and rides off into the sunset singing.

"Oh, give me a home, where the xzerikops roam . . ."

Well, Earthbrain, this is the end. You may have failed this time, but you can always try again. Who knows what strange beings you might meet on your next adventure . . .

95

Suddenly, down through the clouds comes Psili's ship which lands with a bump in the centre of the encampment. The hatch slides open and Psili emerges to lift you from the pot, still steaming.

"Earthbrain, I thought I'd never see you again. If you hadn't activated the homing beacon in the escape pod we couldn't have found you."

"What homing beacon?" you reply, trying to get the herbs out of your ears.

"Why, the button with the flashing red light," says Psili. "Anyway, you're safe now, but not for long if we don't make haste."

Once in the ship you tell him of your adventures and he reveals to you that the rebel android RU12 has plans to destroy all organic life in the galaxy using his army of robots.

Turn to **185**.

96

You slide down until the shaft gradually levels off. Looking around there are junctions and tubes going off in all directions.

After crawling around for hours you're exhausted and completely lost. All the shafts look the same and you've a strange feeling that you're going round and round in circles.

If you have a compass, turn to **74**.
If not, turn to **31**.

97

You look around the tiny cabin of the escape pod. There are banks of dials, rows and rows of buttons and display panels everywhere.

"Surely there must be some food somewhere. I'm starving," you think to yourself. You see a row of important-looking buttons, each with a word above it. The only trouble is that the words are in Gargoid, not the easiest language to understand.

"Oh well, I'd better do something," you think as your finger is poised above the row of buttons. "But which one?"

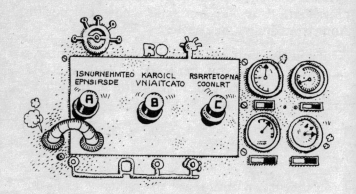

*If you want to press button A, turn to **141**.*
*If you want to press button B, turn to **76**.*
*If you want to press button C, turn to **115**.*

98

You are faced by a horrifying sight, a huge gleaming droid towers over you. It's not just the size of this monster that frightens you. From every part of its huge body there emerge different sorts of limbs. Some with pincers, some with blades, and some with uses that you'd rather not discover.

However, the worst bit by far is where its head should have been. For instead of the normal sort of droid head (which you're getting rather used to), there is what looks like a large goldfish bowl, only in place of a goldfish there's a squirming mass of tentacles.

One of the many arms lifts you clear of the floor and a voice booms, "Come in to my laboratory, Earthling, and let us see if your Earth brain will provide me with an organic matrix to replace this Androxian Megapod." With that, the droid taps its glass dome, causing the tentacles to wriggle.

Turn to **70**.

99

You choose course B and Psili prepares for the jump to light speed. "Strap yourself in good and tight," he says, his yellow finger poised over a large red button. "Here we go."

The engine speed increases and the whole ship is quivering. Psili looks like a lemon jelly on a spin-dryer as the stars change from points of light into multi-coloured streaks.

The quivering stops and Psili unstraps himself. "We're on course for Gargul at light speed," he tells you. "Any moment now we should pick up the homing beacon signal."

Sure enough a few moments later you hear a regular bleeping. "That's it," says Psili with relief, "we'll be back home soon."

Turn to **122**.

100

As you continue, the warble gets louder until you find a steel door with a small grille in it. Looking through the grille you can see Psili sitting on the floor with his head in his hands.

Quickly pulling back the bolts you enter the cell. Psili is overjoyed. "I knew I could rely on you, Earthbrain," he says, as you drag him into the corridor.

"Quickly, there's no time to waste, we must find the ship," you plead.

Turn to **116**.

101

You and Psili are marched off by the droids along passageways and down lifts until you reach a guardroom where a squat droid throws you both into a bare steel cell.

"You'll be here until Lord RU12 is ready for you," the droid says, as the door clangs shut.

Turn to **55**.

102

Having turned off to the left, the pod continues on its way around a gentle curve. As you glance up you see another hoverpod ahead of you. Inside the cabin you recognize a yellow head looking nervously behind.

It's Psili. He slows down a little and as the magnetic couplings of the two carriages make contact, there's a gentle THUNK!

You can relax now, as the pods speed along the tube. In a few moments they begin to slow down as you approach a terminal.

Turn to **48**.

103

"Not a very good start," booms the droid, "perhaps you had better try a little harder, or you'll provide a treat for one of my pets."

At this point you're beginning to think that even the end of term exams are more fun. At least they don't threaten you with a horrible death, just a bad report.

"Couldn't we do the rest of the tests tomorrow?" you ask politely.

The droid reaches out with a huge pincer-like tool and nips off the arm of the chair.

"OK, fine, we'll do them now, if you like," you agree. With that, another strange puzzle appears on the screen.

Which group of shapes makes a perfect circle?

*If you think the answer is A, turn to **45**.*
*If you think the answer is B, turn to **153**.*

104

It's no good, you can't work out the frequency code and the planet is now getting very close.

On the view screen you see a huge portal in the planet surface open like the petals of a flower. The ship is heading straight for it. In a few moments the ship passes through into the interior of the planet Ferrous.

*Turn to **180**.*

105

You're cramped and uncomfortable in the net, but there seems no way to escape.

One of the little creatures reaches through and pinches your arm. It then turns to a companion, jabbering and slapping its lips, whilst rubbing its fat little belly. Even though you don't understand the language, it's easy to guess what they're talking about – Earthling and chips.

Turn to **86**.

106

You decide that it's bearing C. Psili's yellow finger is poised over the fire button, then it plunges down. The torpedo streaks away from the ship, rebounds from the end wall, bounces off the side wall, narrowly missing your ship as it heads for the blast doors.

There is a rather feeble explosion and as the smoke clears you see a small hole in the blast doors.

"Oh dear," says Psili, "it's not as big a hole as I expected. Those photon torpedoes came from Honest Orphlug's War Warehouse on Plato-D. They were an end of season special offer. I've a good mind to take the rest . . ."

Turn to **189**.

107

As you slide into the pilot's couch you gasp in dismay. There's a tangle of wires hanging out of an access panel and a notice which reads 'OUT OF ORDER'. Perhaps you can reconnect them, but which wire goes where?

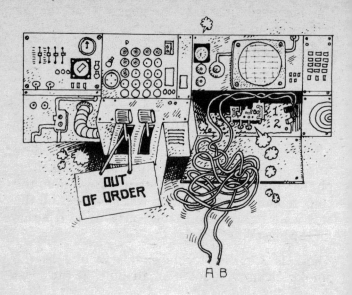

If you think wire A goes to terminal 1, turn to **38**.

If you think wire B goes to terminal 1, turn to **226**.

108

"Oh well, here goes," you think as you press the key. But nothing happens and the door is still firmly shut. With horror you hear the sounds of the Guzzlecruncher recovering and through the gloom you can see its huge form coming towards you.

You flatten yourself against the door as the hideous beast's jaws open wide.

With a jerk the door behind you opens and a steel

hand drags you outside. Turning, you find yourself in the grip of an android. "My master wishes to speak with you, Earthling," it mumbles.

Turn to **131**.

109

As you feel your body beginning to dissolve into separate atoms, you have a strange feeling that something is wrong.

Oh dear, you've got the wrong coordinates. The atoms of your body will drift through space . . . forever.

Well, Earthbrain, this is the end. You may have failed this time, but you can always try again. Who knows what strange beings you might meet on your next adventure . . .

110

Approaching the hooded figure you place your hand upon its shoulder (a rather silly thing to do, in the circumstances). The figure slowly rises and turns, yet you still can't see its face which is hidden in the shadows of the deep hood.

"Why have you come to Mount Dread?" asks a voice from beneath the hood. At this you tell your long and complicated story, of Psili's capture, of your escape and of RU12's plans for destroying all organic life in the galaxy.

The figure nods its head slowly and reaches its gloved hands to the edges of its hood . . .

Turn to **124**.

Feeling in your pocket, you discover a large sticky piece of chewing gum. Falling to the ground, you clutch your stomach and groan. The guard droid leans over to look at you. As he bends forward you thrust the gum into its optical sensor and leap to your feet, pausing just long enough to flick the volume control on his Walkdroid to maximum.

The droid stumbles blindly around, its groping fingers alternately pulling at the sticky gum and trying desperately to remove the ear plug.

You leave the helpless droid and run off down the corridor as fast as you can.

To go back the way you came, turn to **125**.
To run to an open hatch, turn to **132**.

You don't have an idea what to enter. The droid's grip tightens, but with a jerk, a twist and a wriggle (three dances that you're rather good at), you struggle free from its powerful grip, leaving it grasping the tattered remains of your school blazer.

Turn to **27**.

You just can't take the chance that the ship's wings won't go through the hole.

Suddenly Psili screams. "The shields are down," and almost as he says it, there is a tremendous explosion as the droids' blasters hit the main fuel tanks . . . Kerboom . . .

Well, Earthbrain, this is the end. You may have failed this time, but you can always try again. Who knows what strange beings you might meet on your next adventure . . .

114

Turning right at the junction, you continue although your knees are getting rather sore.

Just ahead you see a sign on the shaft wall. It's very old and some of the letters are broken away. However, you try to read it.

If you want to go ahead, turn to **176**.
If you want to turn back, turn to **140**.

Taking a deep breath, you press the button marked C. At first nothing seems to happen, but then you start to feel a bit itchy. Looking down at your hands, you see that they're beginning to become transparent.

Suddenly the words above button C make sense. "Oh no, not again, not the transporter," you scream, as the atoms of your body go zooming off into space for some unknown destination . . .

Turn to **192**.

As you run along the corridor you turn to Psili and gasp, "We must get back to the ship, but how will we find it?"

"That's easy," replies Psili, taking a small black device from one of the many pouches that dangled around his tubby tummy. "It's a Ship Finder. I got it for my last tubeday."

"Don't you mean birthday?" you ask.

"No, we Gargoids aren't born like Earthlings, we're grown in glass tubes. So we celebrate the day that our tube is opened."

Pressing a disc on the smooth surface of the device, Psili turns slowly around until it emits a shrill squeak. You follow the bleeping device through a maze of corridors until, at last, you see the entrance to the docking bay.

Turn to **3**.

117

You understand the sign and hesitate, but just as you are about to raise your arms in surrender, the blast of the droids' photon pistol hits you squarely between the shoulder blades . . .

Well, Earthbrain, this is the end. You may have failed this time, but you can always try again. Who knows what strange beings you might meet on your next adventure . . .

118

Deciding that it's probably safer to run, you swing the controls over and turn the pod away from the approaching ship. Pulling back on the thrust bar, you increase speed until the mystery ship is left far behind you.

For the first time you notice the fuel gauge. The needle is pointing to the red, and there's not a petrol station in sight.

"If I don't find somewhere to land soon, I'll run out of fuel and be drifting in space forever," you think to yourself.

Away to your left you can see a planet and decide to head for it.

Turn to **173**.

119

He sets course for Gargul and you both settle into your flight hammocks.

"Try one of these," he says, offering a small container to you. You look inside to see a mass of what look like tiny blue, wriggling insects.

"But they're alive," you reply in horror.

"Of course they are," says Psili, looking rather surprised, as he pops a handful into his tubular mouth.

Not wishing to appear unfriendly, you dip your hand into the wriggling mass but luckily, just as you're about to face the prospect of actually eating them, a buzzer begins to sound.

Quickly releasing the unwelcome snack, you both turn to the computer screen.

"We've intercepted some sort of message," says Psili. "It's in code."

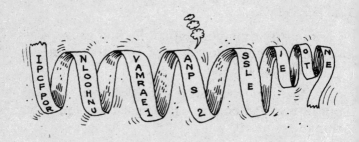

If you can decipher the code, turn to **148**.
If you can't, turn to **154**.

As you pull your hand shakily from your pocket,

something drops to the ground. The huge creature suddenly backs away and rears up with an ear-piercing scream.

You stoop to pick up the object as the Guzzle-cruncher backs terrified into a corner. From the straw at your feet you retrieve a large wobbly, rubber spider. Holding it aloft you approach the cowering beast. With a feeling of power you wobble the spider in the creature's face, and with a throaty gasp, it promptly faints in a heap.

Turn to **160**.

121

As you press the button marked B, there is an ear-splitting shriek as the emergency siren is activated. Ducking behind a nearby shuttle, you see a stream of guard droids rush out of the docking bay to their action stations.

"They must think that Ferrous is being attacked. Let's go while we have a chance," you yell to Psili.

At top speed you both race between the ranks of parked spacecraft until you reach the familiar bulk of Psili's ship.

As you rush up the ramp to the hatch, you notice a large, bright yellow clamp fitted to the forward landing wheel.

Turn to **142**.

122

As the ship approaches the planet Gargul a voice comes through the communication speakers.

"You are entering Gargonian territory. Please identify yourself by using your code signal. If identification is not received within thirty seks, the automatic defence system will be activated."

You notice that Psili is rummaging around. "Now where is that code book? I'm sure I packed it before we left," he mumbles.

On the screen you can see a grid appear. Above it a large red number is rapidly decreasing —30, 29, 28, 27, 26, 25, 24 . . .

"Hurry up and find it," you urge Psili.

"It's no good. It's just disappeared," he replies. Glancing into the corner you see Hoover ripping the pages out of a small book and swallowing them.

"Quick, Psili, Hoover is eating your code book," you cry.

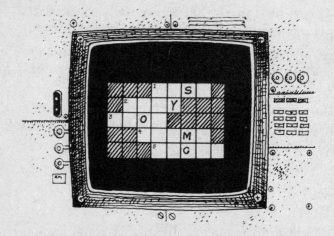

"Oh, you stupid Twit," shouts Psili at the small creature (which is not quite as rude as it sounds), "you've eaten all the pages. You must try to break the code, Earthbrain, or we'll be attacked by my own planet."

Find the identity code.

Clues Across

1. Alive without lungs or legs
2. For mooring boats, a thing that floats
3. Say "after you" when you go through
4. Payment for postage
5. A big dinghy

If you can work out the code, turn to it.
If you can't, turn to **149.**

123

The Gargoid auto-landing system takes over and the ship is guided down through the Gargonian atmosphere.

Psili is getting excited. "Look, look, you can see the lights of the spaceport below," he gasps in delight. "There's the Arrididian Sea, over there, the pink shiny bit."

Slowly the huge spacecraft descends, until it lands with scarcely a bump. "Home at last," says Psili, hopping joyfully out of the hatch.

Turn to **71.**

124

The hood is suddenly thrown back, revealing the glowing eyes and cruel metallic face of an android.

Your arm is gripped in its iron fist as it speaks.

"My master will be well pleased when I return to Ferrous with you, Earthling."

Turn to **178**.

125

As you go along the corridor you hear a familiar warble and head towards the sound.

Turn to **100**.

126

Looking closer, you see that it is some kind of electronic locking device, with a selection of keys to press.

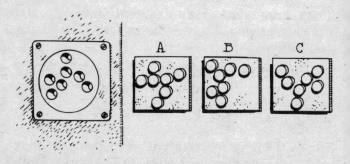

Which key opens the lock?

If it's key A turn to **108**.
If it's key B, turn to **169**.
If it's key C, turn to **68**.

127

Climbing down into the gorge, you begin the perilous crossing. The logs are slippery with spray and you have difficulty keeping your balance.

You are almost across when you come to a gap where the logs don't meet. Gathering your strength, you leap across, just managing to stop from falling into the raging torrent.

A moment later and you're lying gasping on the far bank. After getting your breath back, you climb out of the gorge and head for the strange vehicle. Approaching it carefully you can see that nobody is about.

The hatch is shut and just as you're feeling around it for some kind of handle, a voice behind you drawls, "OK, sidewinder, just reach for the sky and turn around *real* slow . . ."

Turn to **158**.

128

Turning to the right, you shoot off into the maze of tubes. A few moments later you start to think that you must have taken the wrong turning.

A large red sign appears before you, but flashes past almost too quickly for you to read.

Another turning is coming up fast, should you turn left into it or go straight ahead?

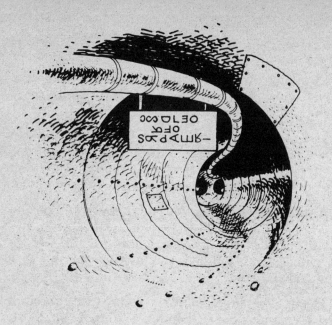

If you want to turn left into the branch tunnel, turn to **54**.
If you want to go straight ahead, turn to **225**.

129

It seems that you're just not taking this adventure seriously. Go back and try again – you won't be let off so lightly next time . . .

Return to **52**.

130

"Spy, spy, spy," they all cry angrily. You're grabbed and dragged out of the door, past the grinning door toad and off deep into the swamp.

"So you think you can fool us, you mechanical moron," says Komyk, giggling as he ties you to an oil-stained wooden stake. "This is what we do with android spies." With that they all depart, giggling and chuckling, leaving you alone . . .

Turn to **166**.

131

You are dragged struggling along a maze of corridors until you reach a vast steel hatch with a guard beside it.

"Here is the Earthbrain that our master has been seeking." The guard droid touches a panel by the hatch and the huge doors shudder and slide apart with a hiss.

Turn to **98**.

132

As you approach the hatch you hear the droid clattering back onto its feet. It's managed to remove the chewing gum and has ripped the plug from its ear.

"Stop or I will terminate you," it warns.

By the open hatchway is a sign. Although you are beginning to understand the droid language, you haven't long to work it out.

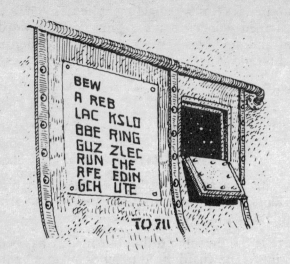

If you want to leap into the open hatch, turn to **192**.

If you don't, turn to **117**.

133

"That'll do," croaks the door toad. "You can go in now." So you knock at the door. Knock! Knock!

"Who's there?" calls a voice.

"An Earthling," you reply.

"An Earthling who?" comes the voice. "Oh, that's no good. It's not funny at all."

With that, the door swings open and there, standing before you, is a very odd-looking being. With a huge grin it stretches out a limb in greeting. "Nice to meet you, to meet you, nice," he chortles. You grasp the 'hand' but drop it quickly as you feel an electric tingle shoot up to your elbow. The creature falls to the floor, tears of mirth streaming down his face. "Just one of my little jests," he gasps between breaths.

After a few minutes he recovers and staggers to his feet, straightening his rather flashy sparkling jacket and bow tie all the while.

"Welcome to Vas Legas, the entertainment capital of the galaxy," he says, still grinning. "Sorry about the quiz show on the doorstep, but we can't be too careful these days."

You smile feebly, "Why did that creature on the door ask me the answer to a joke?" you enquire.

"Well, it's the only way you can tell the difference between organic life-forms and androids. Androids have no sense of humour at all, you know."

You are led along a lavishly-decorated corridor, lined with rows of colourful machines. There's a dreadful wailing music coming from speakers all around. "I left my heart on Delta Phobos . . ." and you're beginning to get a headache.

Turn to **156**.

134

You punch in the code and to your surprise the hatch slides open with a hiss. Once you're inside, the hatch closes behind you, and you turn towards the control console.

Turn to **107**.

You line up the sights on the missile and fire the photon torpedo. Whoosh, the torpedo streaks away towards the fast-approaching missile.

"It's too late to reload," screams Psili. "Let's hope you've chosen the right target." As the torpedo finds its mark, there's a blinding flash and a ball of flame.

At that moment, a different voice comes over the communication speakers.

"This is the Lord High Gargler Phyck. We've just picked up your ship on the visual scanners. Is that you, Commander Psili?"

Psili leaps to the microphone. "Yes, my Lord, it is. My code book was destroyed by a giant android," he says, crossing several of his fingers, "so I couldn't send the identity code."

"Well, you've been identified now," says Phyck, "and you have my permission to land."

Turn to **123**.

Immediately hundreds of tiny monkey-like creatures jump out from the surrounding trees and bushes. They lift you up above their heads and carry you, trussed up like a Christmas turkey, along the jungle paths.

Wondering if you are going to be treated as an enemy or a meal you fail, at first, to notice how old and rotten the net is. Many of the strands are broken. If only you could find a way through . . .

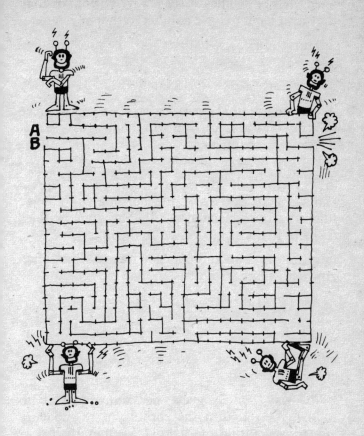

If you think the way through is A, turn to **105**.
If you think the way through is B, turn to **150**.

137

You grab a creeper, but it just falls into a tangled heap at your feet. By the time you grab another, you're surrounded by the tiny jabbering creatures with their blowpipes at the ready. To your dismay they also seem to have another, rather newer net.

Turn to **105**.

138

As the guard droid turns its back on you to place the tray on the floor, you whip your trusty water pistol from your pocket.

He turns just as you send a stream of water directly towards his main circuit panel. With a shower of sparks, a smell of burning and a noise like a vacuum cleaner swallowing your marbles collection, the droid crashes to the floor.

Leaping out into the corridor, you escape, dragging Psili along with you.

Turn to **116**.

139

Creeping along between the rows of ships you come to a corner.

"This way," you suggest, beckoning to Psili to follow. As you turn the corner you're suddenly face to face with a guard droid, his metallic finger already tightening on the trigger of his weapon.

The blast of blue-white light from the photon blaster is the last thing you ever see . . .

Well, Earthbrain, this is the end. You may have failed this time, but you can always try again. Who knows what strange beings you might meet on your next adventure . . .

Despite the dim lighting in the shaft you manage to read the sign and decide to turn back.

As you crawl painfully away from it, you begin to feel a wind tugging at your body. Flattening yourself against the shaft floor you wait until it stops. After a few minutes you continue until you reach a side shaft going off to the right.

Which way now?

If you want to turn right, turn to **36**.
If you want to carry on straight ahead, turn to **56**.

Taking a deep breath you press the button marked A. All that happens is that a small red light starts to blink on and off. You're just about to press one of the other buttons when something catches your eye. On the far side of the cabin is a small chute leading into a bowl-like depression. Above it is just one small lever.

You grab the lever and give it a gentle tug. There's a variety of grinding and slurping noises followed by a loud burp and a small metal canister comes sliding down the chute.

Opening it nervously, you peep inside. It's divided into lots of tiny compartments, each with something that looks like a small white tablet in it. Popping one in your mouth you are disappointed to discover that it doesn't taste of anything at all.

"If only it tasted like sausage and chips," you

think longingly. Suddenly your mouth is full of the exact taste of hot sausage and chips. "That's amazing," you cry in wonder. Grabbing another tablet you concentrate on caramel ripple ice cream with hot chocolate fudge sauce. "Wow, it's incredible."

After a rather strange meal of sausages, ice cream, pineapple, toast, peppermint rock and goldfish (the last one was a mistake, it just popped into your head), you're beginning to feel a little sick. So you settle into the pilot's chair for a rest.

Turn to **42**

142

On closer inspection you find that it's locked on with some kind of combination code. Obviously it was just being fitted when the siren went off as two of the numbers are in position but a third window is

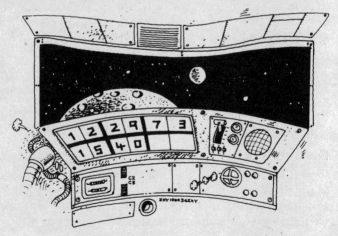

incomplete. Looking down at the third column you try to figure out what the second number must be.

Find the missing number.

If you can work out the number, turn to it.
If you can't, turn to **181**.

143

The laser torpedo speeds off towards its target, but Psili gasps as it appears to pass straight through it. One of the other ships fires its photon cannon at you. The glowing ball of light is heading straight towards your ship.

Turn to **25**.

144

You hook the loop of cable with your foot and pull. Suddenly all the lights go out but as you begin to leap for escape a huge steel pincer grabs your arm.

"Not so fast, Earthling," booms RU12 as he shines a beam of light from one of his arms into your face. "It's just a minor electrical failure. You will be taken to the cells until I discover its cause."

A guard droid is summoned and you are led out into the corridor.

Turn to **91**

Once clear of Ferrous, Psili sets a course for the planet Gargul.

"Well, Earthbrain," says Psili. "With your help I have survived to take news of RU12's plans back to my leader. Perhaps we will yet be in time to prevent the destruction of organic life in our galaxy."

You settle back into the flight hammock and think to yourself that the battle has not yet begun . . .

Turn to **174**.

146

Thanks to your previous efforts in maths lessons (ha ha ha), you are able to work out the missing numbers. Psili manages to block the tractor beam and regains control of the ship.

"Let's get out of here quickly," he yells. "I've just received the sensor scan report and it seems that RU12 is preparing an army. We must return to Gargul and warn them."

Turn to **177**.

147

You set off boldly through the swamp, brushing the swarms of insects away from your face. Although the ground is squelchy, it is fairly solid under your feet.

Deeper and deeper into the jungle you go, pushing aside the branches and hanging creepers and trying to remember the route.

You reach a clearing with several paths leading from it. "Was it left here or straight across and then left," you ponder. "Oh well, I'll try left."

Hour after hour you plod, covered in mud, scratched by sharp thorns and bitten by hordes of hungry insects who obviously think that an Earthling is an unusual treat.

As you're about to give up, you push aside the foliage and see the outline of some strange-looking buildings through the trees. You creep closer, but there's nobody and nothing about, just some steps leading to a big door.

You climb the steps. The big door is bare except for a large knocker in the centre, which is in the shape of a particularly ugly sort of toad-like creature. Grasping the knocker firmly, you are just about to knock when you let go of it in disgust. For instead of being cold and hard (as any civilized person would expect a knocker to be), it is warm and rather clammy. As you stare at it, one of his eyes open and stares back at you.

"Ere, what's your game?" he says in a squeaky croak.

"I was just going to knock at the door, that's all," you reply.

"Well then, I'd be grateful if you'd just keep your hands to yourself."

By this time, both of his eyes are open and staring

at you. "If you want to enter," he continues, "you'll have to answer a question first. I can't go letting just anyone in. For all I know, you might be an android spy."

You're all ready to give your name, date of birth, address and blood group, but the question he asks rather takes you by surprise.

"What's green and hairy, and goes up and down?" asks the door toad, with a very smug expression on his face. "Come on, hurry up, I haven't got all day," he urges.

If it's a Venusian in a temper, turn to **133**.
If it's a gooseberry in a lift, turn to **183**.
If it's a cat on a trampoline, turn to **165**.

148

"This must mean that RU12 is planning something," says Psili.

"Who's 'are you one too'?" you ask.

"Oh, R-U-1-2, he's an android," replies Psili. "He's constructed an artificial planet called Ferrous. We thought it was just a metal-processing plant."

"Then why is he sending messages about invasion plans?" you ask.

"That's just what I think we must try to find out," replies Psili. "I'm setting a course for Ferrous, so we can take a look."

Turn to **170**.

Although you try, you're unable to break the code. The time limit is running out −6, 5, 4, 3 . . .

"What happens if we don't reply?" you ask Psili.

"The defence system will automatically launch the intercept missiles," replies the anxious alien, "and they're coming right now," he adds, pointing to the screen where you can see three slender missiles heading straight for the ship.

"Can't we shoot them down?" you ask, not wanting to give up without a fight.

"We could try, but the Gargoid defence system uses the same method as the Ferrousians. Only one of the missiles is real. The others are holograms to confuse the enemy."

"Quick, increase the screen magnification. Let's see if we can tell which is the real one," you suggest.

Which missile is the odd one out?

If you want to shoot at missile A, turn to **135**.
If you want to shoot at missile B, turn to **190**.
If you want to shoot at missile C, turn to **202**.

Wriggling through the net, you fall to the ground, scattering the tiny jabbering creatures. You leap to your feet and race off down the jungle path with dozens of tiny darts whistling past you as you run.

The pattering of feet follows you down the jungle trail and you hear the excited jabbering of the creatures hot on your scent.

Turn to **207**.

The clouds gradually thin and the tiny craft comes down with a bump. The view screen is misted up so you can't really see what's outside.

With a hiss the hatch slides open, revealing a steamy, swampy jungle.

Turn to **164**.

You decide that it's bearing B. Psili's yellow finger poises over the fire button and plunges down. With a hiss the torpedo streaks away from the ship, hits the far wall, bounces on to the side wall and heads straight towards you.

With a deafening explosion and a ball of fire the ship is reduced to smouldering wreckage . . .

Well, Earthbrain, this is the end. You may have failed this time, but you can always try again. Who knows what strange beings you might meet on your next adventure . . .

You're not really sure whether you want to get the answer right or wrong. But from the angry-looking bubbles frothing in the android's goldfish bowl head, you realize that he's not very pleased.

"I tire of these games," he says in a low menacing whisper. "Are you trying to deceive the great RU12, or are you really stupid?"

If you are really stupid, he's going to feed you to his pets and if you're not, he's going to remove your brain. So you decide that perhaps it's best not to say anything at the moment.

He presses a key and another complex puzzle appears.

How many triangles can you count (including the overlapping ones)?

A = 11
B = 9

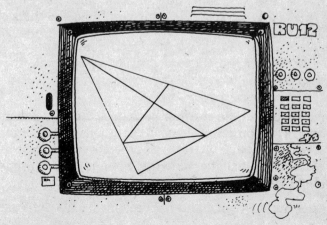

If you think the answer is A, turn to **45**.
If you think the answer is B, turn to **194**.

154

After trying to decipher the code for a while, you decide to give up. In a few moments you begin to doze off to sleep. It's been a long tiring day.

In your dreams you are being shaken by a yellow wobbly alien. As you wake up with a start, you find that you *are* being shaken by a yellow, wobbly alien. "Earthbrain, wake up. Something very strange is happening," pleads Psili. "The ship will not respond to the controls . . ."

Turn to **186**.

155

You sprint through the tangle of wires as the laser bolts explode around you. With a flying dive you reach the safety of the huge speaker.

RU12 realizes that he's beaten and his ship streaks off into space, leaving you lying breathless but alive.

Turn to **195**.

156

At the end of the corridor your host throws open a door and you enter a huge chamber where there seems to be a party in progress. Everyone's wearing silly hats, blowing hooters and falling about laughing.

"Let me introduce you to everyone," says the Vas

Legasian, thrusting a large beaker of smoking blue liquid into your hand. "I'm Komyk, Guardian of The Script and Mirth Master of Vas Legas."

"I'm sorry if I've interrupted your party," you apologize, dodging a runaway balloon.

"Party, what party?" replies Komyk. "This is a meeting of the Grand Council.

"Although you've passed our door guard," he continues, "I don't think we're satisfied yet, especially after your feeble 'knock knock' joke. You could be a new type of android. Where do you come from and what are you doing here on Vas Legas?"

Turn to **59**.

157

"What a contestant," shrieks Komyk, slapping you hard on the back. "Well, I think we're satisfied that you're not an android spy."

With a feeling of relief, you drain the beaker of smoking blue liquid in one swallow and are almost instantly sorry that you did. Your eyes begin to water and your throat burns as the alien brew goes all the way down to your toes.

"Follow me, walk this way. Well, I know you can't walk this way because you've only got two legs," says Komyk. With this, the entire Grand Council collapse in hysterical laughter.

"We have a surprise for you." You try to follow but your legs don't seem to want to go in the same direction as your body . . .

Turn to **18**.

You do as you're told and find yourself looking down at a real wild west cowboy, except for the fact that cowboys aren't usually under three feet tall, or covered in orange fur, or riding something that looks like a giant caterpillar.

"Keep those hands high, you varmint. You won't get the drop on Wire Twerp that easy," he says, falling heavily from his mount onto the ground.

"These dang spurs are always getting caught up on something," he grumbles, brushing the dirt from his leather chaps.

"I had an idea I might have trouble with pesky claim-jumpers," he adds.

"I'm not a claim-jumper," you reply angrily. "I was lost in the forest, saw your vehicle and thought that you might be able to help me. I'm from Earth."

"Earth? Earth? Well, why didn't you say so? You're not from Texas, are you?" asked Wire Twerp eagerly.

"No, I'm from England, Mister Twerp," you reply, "but I don't understand. What's a cowboy doing on Vas Legas?"

"Why, I'm prospecting for trianium crystals. There's a rich seam around here somewhere. But just hold on there, young fella, how do I know you're from Earth? The only thing I know about Earth is from these," he says, reaching into his saddlebag and pulling out a large pile of very worn and dog-eared western comics.

"I found these on some old abandoned spacecraft, I think it was called Pioneer or something. Well, I looked through them and they kinda took my fancy so I made myself this rig," he said proudly, gesturing to his costume.

"If you're really from Earth, as you claim, then you can tell me who invented the revolver."

If you think it was Arthur Remington, turn to **94**.

If you think it was Samuel Colt, turn to **49**.

159

Although there are a few letters at the beginning of the message, the rest is all numbers. What could it mean?

CODE = 3 15 4 5

7, 1, 18, 7, 15, 9, 4   19, 8, 9, 16

8, 5, 1, 4, 9, 14, 7   9, 14, 20, 15

15, 21, 18,   1, 13, 2, 21, 19, 8

If you want to change course, turn to **223**.

If not, turn to **69**.

Strolling casually past the fallen monster, you head for the door which seems to have an illuminated panel beside it.

Turn to **126**.

"What is it?" you scream, above the roar of the engines.

Psili points over your shoulder through the view screen. There is the exit portal, but the blast doors are still firmly shut.

Turn to **203**.

When the electrodes are fitted, he turns to the console where he touches a control pad which activates a bank of flashing lights.

There are loops of cable hanging beneath the control panels. If you stretch, you could just reach them with your foot. His back is turned as you hook the toe of your shoe through a loop of black cable.

Which cable is connected to the power socket?

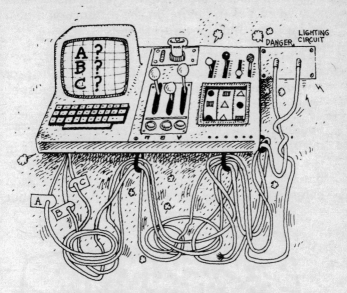

If you want to pull cable A, turn to **179**.
If you want to pull cable B, turn to **144**.
If you want to pull cable C, turn to **82**.

163

The huge menacing jaws are rapidly approaching as you grab the handle on the right and pull it.

Without a moment to spare the ship changes course, narrowly avoiding the mechanical monster.

Turn to **119**.

164

Everywhere you look there are pools of water and boggy-looking patches of ground. The air is buzzing with insects, although they're not insects that you've ever seen before. In the distance you hear odd wailing and chattering sounds.

"There's no point in me just wandering off," you think to yourself. "I'm bound to get lost or drowned in some slimy swamp. But there must be someone around, somewhere out there."

Suddenly you have a brainwave, quite a rare occurence for you. "I know, I'll use the scanner in the escape pod." Climbing back through the hatch, you activate the scanner and on the screen before you appears a sort of map. A flashing dot

shows where the pod has landed and you can see pathways leading through the swamp. Away near the edge of the screen are a cluster of regular shapes which are flashing to show that they contain some sort of energy source. "They look like buildings," you say to yourself hopefully. You look for a route through the swamp from the pod to the buildings.

There's no paper to draw a map on, so you'll just have to remember the way.

Which route will get you out of the swamp?

If you choose route A, turn to **147**.
If you choose route B, turn to **78**.

165

"Wrong," croaks the door toad with a broad grin. With that, the ground below your feet opens up and with a scream, you plummet down, down, down . . .

Well, Earthbrain, this is the end. You may have failed this time, but you can always try again. Who knows what strange beings you might meet on your next adventure . . .

P.S. *If you think that* **165** *is the answer to the problem on* **178**, *you're also wrong. You've obviously forgotten the spare and steering wheels.*
Go back to **178** *and try again.*

166

The twin suns of Vas Legas are beginning to set as you hear the cruel laughter disappearing gradually into the distance.

All around you the jungle is alive with screeches

and growls as its inhabitants come out to hunt.

Suddenly the hair on the back of your neck stands on end. Nearby, in the growing darkness, you can hear something very big slurping through the swamp.

Desperately you pull and tug at the bonds that tie you firmly to the heavy stake, but they're much too strong.

You hear a low throaty growl and see a vast slithering shape getting closer.

If you have a penknife, turn to **92**.
If not, turn to **184**.

167

At last you reach the mountain top. It's a wild and desolate place and the wind is howling and tearing at the tattered remains of your school uniform.

Scrambling onto a wide ledge you see the dark entrance to a cave.

"Well, at least it'll be a bit warmer in there," you think as you tiptoe into the entrance. Exploring a little further you come to a passageway and this splits into two tunnels.

You must decide which way to go.

If you want to go left, turn to **230**.
If you want to go right, turn to **199**.

168

You take a deep breath and say to Psili, "Come on, let's go for it."

His hand closes over the thrust lever, the ship rises a few feet, spins round and heads for the hole in the doors.

At the last moment you wonder if you've made the right choice, but Psili tilts the ship on its side and it just scrapes through the opening.

Turn to **145**.

169

Try as you might, you just can't open the door. As you continue to try the various buttons, a sound behind you makes your hair start to prickle.

Spinning round, you find yourself face to face with the Black Slobbering Guzzlecruncher . . . Aaarrrggghhh!!!

Well, Earthbrain, this is the end. You may have failed this time, but you can always try again. Who knows what strange beings you might meet on your next adventure . . .

170

After some time Psili announces that you are approaching Ferrous. "Look," he says, "you can see it on the scanners. Hold on though, what's that?"

On the screen between your ship and the planet, you can see some rapidly-moving dots.

"Looks like a welcoming committee," says Psili. As he increases magnification, you can clearly see

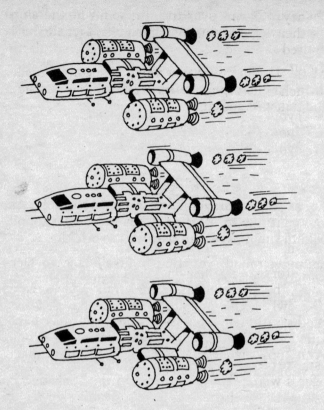

that there are three ships. Suddenly a glowing ball of light shoots from one of them and narrowly misses the ship.

"They're firing photon cannons at us," yells Psili, "but the sensors indicate that there is only one ship. The other two are holograms. It's an old trick. We've only got one laser torpedo ready to fire and a few seconds to fire it in."

"How do we tell which is the real one?" you ask. Psili quickly increases magnification to maximum.

"They look almost exactly the same, but only one of them can destroy us," he cries, as his hand is poised over the FIRE button. "You choose, Earth-brain."

Which ship is the odd one out?

If you think it's ship A, turn to **204**.
If you think it's ship B, turn to **196**.
If you think it's ship C, turn to **143**.

171

You decide that it's bearing A. Psili's yellow finger is poised over the fire button, then plunges down.

The torpedo streaks off, rebounds from the end wall, bounces off the side wall and screams narrowly past your ship, heading for the blast doors.

There is a tremendous explosion and, as the smoke clears, you see a vast gaping hole where the doors were. Psili pulls back on the controls, the ship rises a little, spins round and streaks off through the opening.

Turn to **145**.

172

As the huge shambling creature approaches, you see an evil glint from between its dribbling jaws and from its mean little red eyes.

Although you might not appreciate it, you're quite a celebrity, the very first Earthling to be eaten by a Black Slobbering Guzzlecruncher. However, there's not really time to contact *The Guinness Book of Records* because what the BSG lacks in table manners it certainly makes up for in punctuality – especially at mealtimes.

Well, as the rest of the Universe is about to find out, Earthlings, puny and feeble though they might be, don't give up without a fight.

You frantically search your pockets for a weapon, but even the Swiss army don't have a gadget on their penknives for tackling an elephant-sized carnivore.

If you have a rubber spider, turn to **120**.
If you don't, turn to **89**.

173

As the planet gets closer, you can see that it's surrounded by thick clouds.

"That means it's probably like Earth and rains all the time," you grumble. "Still it'll be jolly good to get my feet on solid ground for a change."

You ease the controls forward and the tiny pod gently sinks through the thick clouds . . .

Turn to **151**.

174

"There's no time to waste. We must get back to Gargul quickly and that means we must travel at light speed," explains Psili.

Turn to **84**.

Taking a deep breath you turn to Psili. "I'm staying. If we're in danger, we'll face it together," you say (just like a hero out of a story book).

"I've just got the data through," cries Psili, pointing to the screen. "We're being pulled towards the planet Ferrous. It must be some kind of a tractor beam," he adds, his yellow skin going slightly greenish. "If the computer can work out the frequency of the transmission we may be able to block it."

In his panic to reach the controls he trips over the computer input lead, ripping it out of its socket. "Quick, Earthbrain, the computer has calculated the first part of the frequency code, you'll have to complete it in your head."

Number of days in a leap year ÷ 6 + number of weeks in a year + 33 = ?

Find the missing number.

If you can work out the missing number, turn to it.

If you can't, turn to **104**.

176

You decide to go ahead. Perhaps it's an exit of some kind. It's strange, but you seem to feel a wind blowing and it's getting stronger all the time.

You're getting blown along the shaft now, faster and faster. As you pop out of the airlock, like a cork out of a bottle, you catch a glimpse of another sign – Danger Ventilation Exhaust.

You're floating in space, drifting further from the salvage droid and you can't hold your breath any longer . . .

Well, Earthbrain, this is the end. You may have failed this time, but you can always try again. Who knows what strange beings you might meet on your next adventure . . .

177

Psili sets a course for Gargul and increases the thrust. "We'll have to get clear of this belt of asteroids before we can change to light speed," says Psili, surrounded by the glowing instrument panels.

"Just a moment, we've intercepted a message. It's not in normal droidspeak. Perhaps it's some kind of battle code."

After running it through the computers, Psili still can't understand the message.

"Here, Earthbrain, you try," he says, handing you the printout.

You look hard at the message, which is just a mass of numbers.

Turn to **159**.

178

You are dragged protesting through the tunnels and down a steep mountain path. Far below you can see a sinister black spacecraft poised on a wide ledge of rock.

You slip your hands into your pockets to protect them from the biting cold mountain air and with surprise feel a smooth, flat, rectangular object.

Number of wheels a car has
X 20 + 91 — Number of legs
on an insect = ?

When you reach the ship you are thrown into a small cabin while the droid prepares to take off. Quickly you pull the object from your pocket. It's the control pad from the escape pod's teleporter.

If only you can remember the correct coordinates. You remember the formula but can you work out the answer? Knowing that a horrible fate awaits you on Ferrous, you decide to take a chance and enter the coordinates into the control pad.

You feel the familiar tingling sensation as your atoms are beamed out into space . . .

Find the missing number.

> *If you can work out the coordinate, turn to it.*
> *If not, turn to* **109**.

179

As you pull the cable, there's a huge explosion. The console at which RU12 stands is torn apart and the huge droid is blasted back against the wall.

You tear the electrodes from your head and leap to the door, sprinting off down the corridor at top speed.

After running for several minutes, you hear a familiar warble and head towards the sound.

> *Turn to* **100**.

180

The ship travels down a dark tunnel for some time, the steel walls barely visible in the gloom.

Suddenly, there's light ahead as a vast circular opening appears, and the ship passes into a brightly-lit docking bay.

Psili turns to you as the ship settles gently onto a landing pad.

"Now, Earthbrain, you are about to see something that few beings have been priviliged to see. A secret that we Gargoids have guarded for aeons — the awesome power of Gargoid Mind Control."

At that moment the hatch opens to reveal a squad of menacing androids, their armoured bodies glinting blue-black in the light.

The largest, its crested head towering high above you, approaches. "The Lord RU12 sends his welcome, and bids that you accept his hospitality," he says in a voice more suited to a cartoon character than to something out of a horror comic. "I am Darpht Ada, Centurian of the Guard. You will follow me."

At that moment Psili hops forward, drawing his flexible body to its full height — slightly above the droid's knee level. He stretches his fingers and focuses all his eyes on the droid's optical sensor. In a mystical warble he begins to speak.

"You will release us," he intones. "You will forget our very existence and allow us to leave in peace."

The huge droid leans forward slowly, plucks Psili from the ground, lifting him until his optical sensor is level with Psili's cluster of startled eyes. "Cease these games, Gargoid fool," he growls, dropping the startled Psili in a heap at his feet.

"It usually works," says Psili apologetically, as you all follow the droids down the ramp to the floor of the docking bay.

If you have any marbles, turn to **188**.
If not, turn to **101**.

181

You are both crouching by the clamp, desperately trying to open it, when you hear a noise behind you.

Turning, you find that the droids have returned to the docking bay, having discovered that the siren was a false alarm.

You run for cover, but it's too late. You're spotted and you don't even see the blast of light from their weapons as they reduce you and Psili to a small pile of smoking ash . . .

Well, Earthbrain, this is the end. You may have failed this time, but you can always try again. Who knows what strange beings you might meet on your next adventure . . .

Player's Note: *Here's a clue to the puzzle. 12+1+2 =15, 29+2+9=40 – now complete the sequence.*

182

As you answer, the droid reaches for the lever. "I'm sorry, Earthling, but you have failed." The lever comes down with a clang. The seat of the couch on which you are sitting disappears and you're falling.

With a thud you land in a small steel chamber. Perhaps the fall has made you dizzy, but you have a weird feeling that the walls are closing in.

Oh dear, it's not a weird feeling at all, they are closing in . . . crunch!

Well, Earthbrain, this is the end. You may have failed this time, but you can always try again. Who knows what strange beings you might meet on your next adventure . . .

183

"That'll do," croaks the door toad. "You can go in now." So you knock at the door. Knock! Knock!

"Who's there?" calls a voice.

"An Earthling," you reply.

"An Earthling who?" comes the voice. "Oh, that's not funny at all."

With that, the door swings open and there, standing before you, is a very odd-looking being. With a huge grin he stretches out a limb in greeting. "Nice to meet you, to meet you, nice," he chortles. You grasp the 'hand' but drop it quickly as you feel an electric tingle shoot up to your elbow. The creature falls to the floor, tears of mirth streaming down his face. "Just one of my little jests," he gasps between breaths.

After a few minutes he recovers and staggers to his feet, straightening his rather flashy sparkling jacket and bow tie.

"Welcome to Vas Legas, the entertainment capital of the galaxy," he says, still grinning.

"Sorry about the quiz show on the doorstep, but we can't be too careful these days."

You smile feebly. "Why did that creature on the door ask me the answer to a joke?" you enquire.

"Well, it's the only way you can tell the difference between organic life-forms and androids. Androids have no sense of humour at all, you know."

You are led along a lavishly-decorated corridor, lined with rows of colourful machines. There is a dreadful wailing sound coming from speakers all around, 'I left my heart on Delta Phobos . . .', and you're beginning to get a headache.

Turn to **156**.

184

It's getting closer. You can see its huge lizard-like head with a long forked tongue flicking to and fro.

The strong bonds resist your efforts to break free. You feel the monster's hot breath on your cheek as it opens its vast mouth . . . and closes it . . . crunch!

Well, Earthbrain, this is the end. You may have failed this time, but you can always try again. Who knows what strange beings you might meet on your next adventure . . .

185

Psili slips into the control couch. "We must return to Gargul as fast as possible to warn my leader of the coming invasion."

You strap yourself in and, with a tremendous roar, the ship streaks away. Travelling at thousands of kilometres a second the journey doesn't take very long.

Turn to **122**.

186

"I've tried everything but the controls are completely dead. Some kind of force has taken over the ship," continues the worried Gargoid. He turns to the computer screen. "At least I can try to find out where we're going . . ."

After a moment, Psili turns to you, "Look, Earthbrain, you must take the escape pod and try to get away, there's only room for one."

"I can't leave you," you reply bravely.

"You must," urges Psili. "I think we're in grave danger. But it's your choice, I can't force you."

"What a choice," you think to yourself. "Stay with Psili and face the unknown or set off in the tiny escape pod . . . alone . . ."

If you want to stay with Psili, turn to **175**.
If you want to take the escape pod, turn to **93**.

187

The hoverpods gather speed as they streak along in the tubes. You can see Psili's yellow head wobbling about in the carriage ahead of you.

Hoover is leaping about excitedly, when he

suddenly loses his balance and falls onto the controls of the hoverpod.

The little pod lurches and separates from Psili's vehicle. Suddenly you look ahead and see that the tube branches into two. Psili's pod goes in one direction whilst yours zooms off in the other . . .

Turn to **200**.

188

As you walk down the sloping ramp, your hand slips into your pocket and feels the marbles. With a sudden movement you roll them along the smooth floor towards the squad of droids.

The droids rush forwards, stepping on the marbles. They stumble and crash into one another as their gyros whirr in an effort to keep their feet on the ground.

Taking your chance to escape, you sprint to the docking bay exit. You can hear the droids following, but the sound of Psili's yellow foot has disappeared.

As you turn into a corridor you can hear the sounds of the droids getting closer. Looking around you see a grille in the wall, which you pull away to reveal a smooth shaft.

Just as the droids round the bend and raise their weapons, you dive into the shaft.

Turn to **96**.

189

"Oh, do shut up," you complain. "You won't get your money back if we don't get out of here. Quickly, what's the wingspan of this ship?" you ask.

"It's exactly 700 yarl," replies Psili, "and a yarl is about equal to sixty of your Earth millimetres."

You look at the hole in the blast doors, it looks about fifty metres across – will the ship get through it?

> If you think that the ship will get through, turn to **168**.
> If you don't, turn to **79**.

190

You line up the sights on the missile and fire the photon torpedo. Whoosh, the torpedo streaks away but passes straight through the fast-approaching missile.

"It's too late to reload," screams Psili, as one of the other missiles finds its target.

There's a blinding flash, then nothing . . .

Well, Earthbrain, this is the end. You may have failed this time, but you can always try again. Who knows what strange beings you might meet on your next adventure . . .

191

You quickly gather the equipment together and set off with Psili in the hoverpods.

You are heading for the zone where you think that RU12's fleet is going to land.

Turn to **9**.

192

Crash! You land in a crumpled heap, stunned, lying on your back with your eyes closed.

Gradually you open them painfully and look around. You're lying in a big dimly-lit chamber, the floor strewn with something like straw.

Wriggling to ease the pain in your back, you realize that you're lying on something hard which, to your horror, seems to be a bone.

As you recover your senses and struggle to your feet, you become aware of a strange fetid stench. A muffled shuffling sound at the far end of the chamber turns you rigid with terror. What can it be. . . ?

The shuffling gets louder and a low throaty growling adds to your fears.

Gradually, through the gloom, you can make out the outline of a huge shaggy something . . . coming towards you . . .

Turn to **172**.

193

You think you've found the damaged circuit and quickly repair it. Just as you're about to test the system, a messenger rushes in.

"We've just picked up signals of a large fleet of ships approaching Gargul," he announces breathlessly.

Turn to **211**.

194

One of the massive droid's huge fists crashes down on the control console. The whole room trembles as he roars, "Why, the Slime Worms of Trialus have more brains than you, Earthling. I'll give you one final chance. How many bones do you Earthlings have in your pathetic bodies?"

If it's **206**, *turn to* **206**.
If it's **182**, *turn to* **182**.

195

As if from nowhere, crowds of Gargoids suddenly appear. You are lifted shoulder high and carried back to the council chamber.

There, amidst banqueting and celebrations, you are awarded the medal of the Order of Garglers, Gargul's highest military honour.

Psili takes you to one side and whispers in your ear, "I have not forgotten the promise I made you when we first met." Saying that, he presses a small, black rectangular box into your hand. "It's a transmuter," he continues, "follow the instructions and use it with care."

Turn to **219**.

One of Psili's many fingers comes down on the FIRE button and you see the laser torpedo speeding towards its target.

You shield your eyes at the brilliant ball of fire as the Ferrous scout ship explodes into a billion pieces. At the same moment the two other ships dissolve into nothingness.

"Good work," Psili warbles. "Had you not chosen the right ship to attack, we'd be a few atoms floating in space by now." Moments later, Psili points to a gigantic gleaming sphere on the view screen. "Look, we're approaching Ferrous now. You can see it on the scanner. We don't want to get too close," he adds, settling in the control couch. "I'll put the ship into orbit."

His face, which usually looked a bit odd, was looking odder than usual.

"What's the trouble?" you ask the worried Gargoid.

"It's the ship. It won't respond to the controls . . ."

Turn to **175**.

You climb up a ladder and peep over the cockpit of the shuttle. At the far end of the docking bay, near the exit portal, you can see the familiar shape of Psili's ship. But between you and the ship are row upon row of other spacecraft. Some are parked so

close together that there is no room to get between them. There are lots of guard droids
patrolling up and down with their photon blasters
at the ready.

Climbing down, you turn to Psili and tell him the
problem.

"I think I can remember the route we must follow
to avoid the droids," you tell him as you set off.

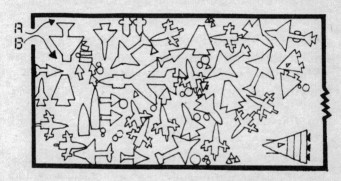

Which route will take you safely through the
docking bay?

If you want to follow route A, turn to **139**.
If you want to follow route B, turn to **210**.

198

Climbing down into the gorge, you begin the
perilous crossing. The logs are slippery with spray
and you have difficulty keeping your balance.

You are almost across when you come to a gap

where the logs don't meet. Gathering your strength, you leap across the gap but your foot slips on the treacherous surface and you plunge into the raging torrent.

Gasping for breath, you swim to the bank but the rocks are too smooth and slippery. You can't get a grip and are washed away down the river.

Your strength is failing, you feel yourself being sucked down, your mouth fills with water ... glug!

Well, Earthbrain, this is the end. You may have failed this time, but you can always try again. Who knows what strange beings you might meet on your next adventure ...

199

You wander along the dark stone passages, passing countless tunnel entrances along the way. Deciding that you've had enough, you turn to go back to the entrance only to find that you're completely lost.

You search for hour after hour, but all the tunnels look just the same.

If you have some chalk, turn to **63**.
If not, turn to **215**.

200

Pushing Hoover out of the way, you look at the control panel. The controls are very simple to operate, but there is a terribly complex map on the screen.

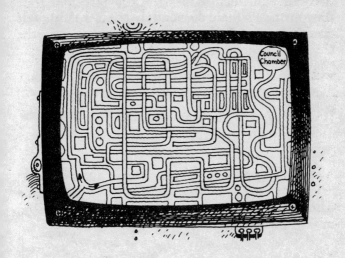

The map shows the complete hoverpod system that runs around the city of Gargoplex. It's a tangled mass of tubes, passing over and under each other as they weave around the sprawling city.

You know that Psili was heading for the council chamber of the Lord High Gargler, but which route will take you there?

At that moment you see another junction approaching. You must decide which way to go, quickly.

Which route will take you to the council chamber?

If you want to go right, turn to **128**.
If you want to go left, turn to **102**.

As you and Psili are desperately trying to untangle the wires, a sound makes you look up into the sky. There, hovering high above your heads, is a vast battle fleet.

"Quick, the wires," you cry. "We must get them connected."

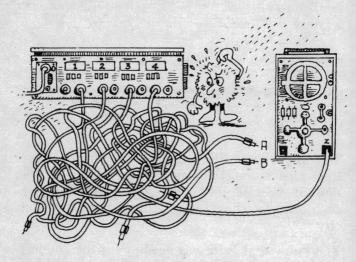

Which wire connects socket 1?

If you think wire A goes into socket 1, turn to **16**.

If you think wire B goes into socket 1, turn to **22**.

202

You line up the sights on the missile and fire the photon torpedo. Whoosh, the torpedo streaks away, but passes straight through the fast-approaching missile.

"It's too late to reload," screams Psili, as one of the other missiles finds its target.

There's a blinding flash, then nothing . . .

Well, Earthbrain, this is the end. You may have failed this time, but you can always try again. Who knows what strange beings you might meet on your next adventure . . .

203

"We can't open the doors," says Psili grimly. "So we'll just have to go through them."

"But how?" you ask. "The ship will be wrecked."

"Load the photon torpedo tube and I'll show you," replies Psili. "The only problem is that, as the ship is facing the wrong way, we'll have to use a

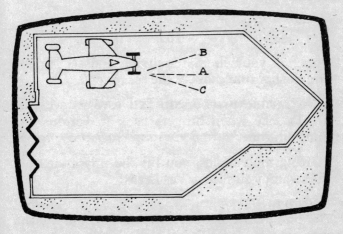

delayed charge and bounce the torpedo off the walls back to the blast doors. You must work out the bearing for me, so that the torpedo hits the doors and not us."

You look down at the screen which shows a plan of the docking bay. There are three alternative bearings but which one will hit the doors?

If you think it's A, turn to **171**.
If you think it's B, turn to **152**.
If you think it's C, turn to **106**.

204

The laser torpedo speeds off towards its target, but Psili gasps as it appears to pass straight through it.

One of the other ships fires its photon cannon at you. The glowing ball of light is heading straight at your ship.

Turn to **25**.

205

You feel yourself materializing and see around you the familiar cabin of the escape pod.

You chuckle to yourself, "I'd love to see that droid's face when he gets back to Ferrous and finds I'm gone."

Starting the engines, you lift the tiny craft from the swampy surface of Vas Legas.

Turn to **87**.

As your mind races, you see one of RU12's many hands reach for a lever. But on hearing your answer his hand moves slowly away from it.

Turn to 75.

Suddenly you burst through the undergrowth and find yourself on the bank of a swiftly-flowing river. The sounds of the pursuing creatures is getting louder.

A B C

The river is too dangerous to try to swim across but hanging from the trees above your head are long creepers. They're knotted and tangled but strong enough to carry your weight.

Saying to yourself, "Well, if Tarzan can do it so can I", you grab one and launch yourself into the air.

"AAaaRRrrAAa . . ."

Which creeper will let you swing across the river?

If you choose creeper A, turn to **137**.
If you choose creeper B, turn to **28**.
If you choose creeper C, turn to **224**.

208

The next morning it's back to school and, would you believe it, a double maths period with Hardgraft, your least favourite teacher.

You manage to survive through the lesson until it's time to hand in your homework. As you place the book on the master's desk and walk towards the door, a voice rings out.

"You boy, back here."

Head hung low, you walk back. "What's all this?" he says, pointing to your maths homework. "You didn't do this, it's perfect. Who did you copy it from? Either you tell me or it's down to the head with you."

With a sweet smile you tell him, "I used my new calculator. It was a present," taking a small, black rectangular box from your pocket.

"You're not allowed to use calculators for homework, boy," the master bellows.

"Oh, this one's different," you reply, pointing the box at him and pressing a button.

You walk from the room with a broad smile on your face. As you stroll away down the corridor you hear a boy's voice shout in the distance. "Hey, look at this, one of the frogs has escaped from the biology lab. We'd better catch it. We're doing dissection after lunch . . ."

THE END

209

You quickly gather the equipment together and set off with Psili in the hoverpods. You're heading for the zone where you think RU12's battle fleet is going to land.

Turn to **9**.

210

Creeping along between the rows of ships, you manage to avoid the patrolling droids.

Eventually you reach Psili's ship. Luckily, there isn't a guard in sight. But as you rush up the ramp to the main hatch, you notice that a large bright yellow clamp has been fitted to the forward landing wheel.

Turn to **142**.

211

You gather the equipment together and set off with Psili to the area where you think RU12's battle fleet is going to land. When you arrive, you find that the wires have got terribly tangled during the journey.

As you and Psili are desperately trying to untangle the wires, a sound makes you look up to the sky. There, hovering high above your heads, is a vast fleet of battleships.

"Quick the wires," you cry. "We must get them connected."

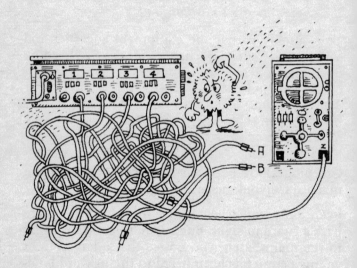

Which wire goes to socket 1?

If you think wire A goes into socket 1, turn to **13**.

If you think wire B goes into socket 1, turn to **22**.

212

"OK," says Psili, "let's do it, quick." You both leap to disconnect the wiring and move the heavy speakers. In a few moments they are pointing in the other direction. As you're gathering the wires you both look up.

There in the sky is a vast battle fleet, coming down rapidly through the clouds.

"Quickly, Psili, get the wires plugged in. There isn't a moment to spare," you yell.

Turn to **16**.

213

You're beginning to get worried. "They should have been here by now," you say, turning to Psili. You're both standing staring into the sky above the landing zone, but there's nothing in sight.

"Perhaps we're in the wrong zone," suggests Psili. "You did the calculations in an awful hurry."

"You could be right," you agree, "but if we go back to check the figures, they may arrive before we're ready for them."

If you want to stay, turn to **15**.
If you want to go back and check, return to **5**.

214

Looking down into the river below, you notice that there are many tree trunks washed down during floods.

They're jammed against the rocky river bed and, although the river is wide and fast-flowing, it may be possible to find a route across the logs to the other side.

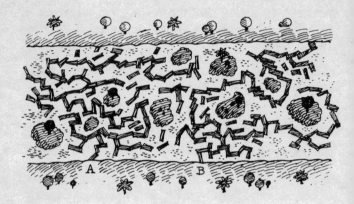

Which route will allow you to safely cross the river (you may only cross where the logs are touching)?

If you choose route A, turn to **198**.
If you choose route B, turn to **127**.

215

Exhaustion finally overcomes you and you sink to the cold stone floor.

What adventures you would have been able to tell your friends about – if you had survived to return.

Well, Earthbrain, this is the end. You may have failed this time, but you can always try again. Who knows what strange beings you might meet on your next adventure . . .

You gather the equipment together and set off with Psili to the area where you think RU12's battle fleet is going to land. When you arrive, you find that the wires have got terribly tangled during the journey.

Turn to **201**.

Coming over the crest of a small hill are hordes of heavily-armed droids.

"Oh no!" cries Psili, "we are in the wrong zone. They've landed behind us. The speakers are facing the wrong way."

Leading the army is a huge Ferrousian Warbot, its blue-black armour glinting in the sunlight.

He raises a photon cannon and a blinding beam of light streaks towards you. Moments later you and Psili are lying lifeless amongst the tangled wires . . .

Well, Earthbrain, this is the end. You may have failed this time, but you can always try again. Who knows what strange beings you might meet on your next adventure . . .

At first there's no reaction. Then the droids pause, wisps of smoke appear around them, they scrabble at their heads. Suddenly the air is full of crackling, popping sounds and the smell of burning rubber, as a billion circuits begin to overload.

One by one the droids totter and fall to the ground. Except for one. The mighty RU12 isn't affected, as his brain is partly organic. As he climbs into the cockpit of his waiting craft, he points one of his steel fingers at you, and growls in a low and threatening voice.

"Earthbrain, I, RU12, will not forget you. I will return to seek vengeance on you and the peoples of your puny planet."

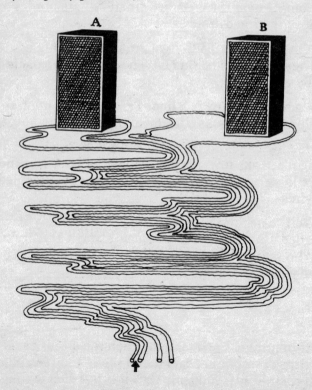

With the threat still ringing in your ears, his craft slowly lifts into the air. Suddenly it swings towards you with lasers firing. You run for the shelter of one of the huge speakers, but can you get through the tangle of wires. . . ?

If you can reach speaker A, turn to **155**.
If you can reach speaker B, turn to **229**.

219

You suddenly begin to feel very homesick. It's been a long time since you saw Earth. Turning to Psili, you tell him your feelings.

"Well, we'll be sorry to see you go," sniffs the Gargoid, wiping away a tear, "but I suppose you're right." He leads you into the transporter room, where you realize the terrible mess you are in.

"I can't go home looking like this," you say, gazing down at the tattered remains of your school uniform.

"Don't worry, we'll soon fix that," says Psili, taking the transmuter from you. He points the small box at your ruined clothes and presses a few buttons. Zap! Instantly you look like you've just stepped out of a shop window.

"Thank you and goodbye," you say, hugging the wobbly yellow body. Then you step into the transporter.

Psili activates the beam and enters your home coordinates. "Remember, you've been travelling at light speed, so when you get back it will only be a few minutes after the time you left," he shouts.

The last thing you see is his yellow waving hand, as you feel yourself disappearing . . .

Turn to **10**.

220

As you pull lever C, you hear Psili's voice behind you.

"Not that one, it's the transporter . . ."

. . . Moments later you're back on Earth. It's a wet Monday morning and you've got a double maths period to look forward to.

If only you'd learned to read Gargoid, just think of the adventures you might have had . . .

Well, Earthbrain, this is the end. You may have failed this time, but you can always try again. Who knows what strange beings you might meet on your next adventure . . .

221

From your pocket you pull a bar of chocolate that's looking a little worn. The wrapper's coming off and you have to pick bits of fluff from its sticky surface before you can eat it.

Still, it's better than nothing.

Turn to **42**.

222

As you press the button the compartment shoots

upwards at an alarming rate, leaving your stomach far below.

Eventually it slows down and comes to a stop. As you step out into the corridor you hear a familiar warble and follow the sound.

Turn to **100**.

223

"Change course – now," you yell at Psili. "We're heading into an ambush. I've just discovered what the code means."

With that Psili swings the controls and the ship banks into an emergency turn.

Turn to **84**.

224

You swing majestically across the raging river, leaving the tiny jabbering creatures stamping and hungry on the bank behind.

Landing with a bump you look around to see a strange vehicle standing nearby. There's nobody in sight as you creep up to it. Suddenly a voice drawls behind you, "OK, sidewinder, just reach for the sky and turn around *real* slow . . ."

Turn to **158**.

225

You decide to go straight ahead. The tiny pod is streaking along down the tube approaching a bend. As you round the bend you see to your horror that the tube comes to a sudden end.

"Oh no, that sign must have said that this tube is closed for repairs," you scream. Applying the brakes, the pod begins to slow down, but it's much too late . . . crash!

Well, Earthbrain, this is the end. You may have failed this time, but you can always try again. Who knows what strange beings you might meet on your next adventure . . .

226

It's no good, the wires are so tangled it's impossible to see which one goes where. You'll just have to leave the escape pod, go back into the ship and await your fate with Psili.

Back in the main cabin you're just in time to see the massive steel jaws close, engulfing the ship . . .

Turn to **180**.

227

As you approach the hatch you hear the droid clattering back to its feet. "Stop or I will terminate you," it warns.

By the open hatchway is a sign. Although you are beginning to understand the droid language, you haven't long to work it out.

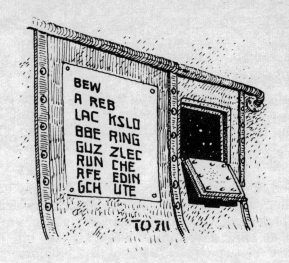

BEW
A REB
LAC KSLO
BBE RING
GUZ ZLEC
RUN CHE
RFE EDIN
GCH UTE
TO 7II

If you want to leap into the open hatch, turn to
192.
If you don't, turn to **117**.

228

"Thank goodness I've learned to read a little
Gargoid," you gasp, as you step back nervously
from the fence. "There are enough problems to
deal with already, without ending up as the main
course in a plant's dinner."

You decide to go back to your quarters and try to
think of a plan.

Turn to **8**.

229

As you sprint through the tangle of wires, your foot catches in a loop and you crash to the ground.

Struggling to your feet you see RU12's ship diving towards you, lasers blasting. You try to run, but your feet are still caught. The next blast from the laser hits you and you slump down into the tangled wires . . .

Well, Earthbrain, this is the end. You may have failed this time, but you can always try again. Who knows what strange beings you might meet on your next adventure . . .

230

Setting off again you soon find yourself at the entrance to a massive chamber with a high vaulted ceiling. Glancing around the room, you see at the far end a figure sitting on a block of carved stone.

You call, "Hello there, hooded figure," but there's no reply so you walk boldly, but perhaps rather stupidly, towards the figure whose head is completely covered by the hood of a long flowing cloak . . .

Turn to **110**.

To help you keep a track of where you have been during your adventure, note the section numbers on the Tracking Sheet.

SECTION	SECTION	SECTION	SECTION	SECTION
SECTION	SECTION	SECTION	SECTION	SECTION
SECTION	SECTION	SECTION	SECTION	SECTION
SECTION	SECTION	SECTION	SECTION	SECTION
SECTION	SECTION	SECTION	SECTION	SECTION
SECTION	SECTION	SECTION	SECTION	SECTION
SECTION	SECTION	SECTION	SECTION	SECTION
SECTION	SECTION	SECTION	SECTION	SECTION
SECTION	SECTION	SECTION	SECTION	SECTION
SECTION	SECTION	SECTION	SECTION	SECTION
SECTION	SECTION	SECTION	SECTION	SECTION
SECTION	SECTION	SECTION	SECTION	SECTION
SECTION	SECTION	SECTION	SECTION	SECTION

SECTION	SECTION	SECTION	SECTION	SECTION
SECTION	SECTION	SECTION	SECTION	SECTION
SECTION	SECTION	SECTION	SECTION	SECTION
SECTION	SECTION	SECTION	SECTION	SECTION
SECTION	SECTION	SECTION	SECTION	SECTION
SECTION	SECTION	SECTION	SECTION	SECTION
SECTION	SECTION	SECTION	SECTION	SECTION
SECTION	SECTION	SECTION	SECTION	SECTION
SECTION	SECTION	SECTION	SECTION	SECTION
SECTION	SECTION	SECTION	SECTION	SECTION
SECTION	SECTION	SECTION	SECTION	SECTION
SECTION	SECTION	SECTION	SECTION	SECTION
SECTION	SECTION	SECTION	SECTION	SECTION

GRAIL QUEST

Solo Fantasy Gamebooks

J. H. Brennan

King Arthur's magic realm of Avalon is besieged on every side by evil powers and foul monsters. You alone can free the kingdom from its terror, venturing forth on Quests too deadly for even the bold Knights of the Round Table. Quests that will lead you to glory — or death.

So sharpen your wits and your trusty sword Excalibur Junior, and use the intricate combat system to scheme and fight your way through the adventures in this thrilling gamebook series. A special score card and detachable easy-reference rules bookmark are included with each book.

The Castle of Darkness	**The Den of Dragons**
The Gateway of Doom	**Voyage of Terror**
Kingdom of Horror	**Realm of Chaos**
Tomb of Nightmares	**Legion of the Dead**

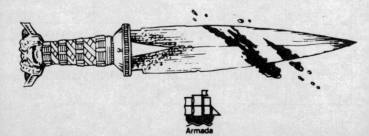

Armada

Horror Classic Gamebooks
by J. H. Brennan

Now you can bring your favourite horror characters
to life in these spinechilling gamebooks.

Dracula's Castle

Deadly traps and evil cunning await Jonathan Harker on
his arrival at the forbidding Castle Dracula. The choice
is yours whether to play the fearless vampire-hunter or
his arch-enemy, the vampire count himself. Will you
have the stamina to survive?

The Curse of Frankenstein

Enter the ghoulish world of Frankenstein and his
monstrous creation. But be warned, you will need skill,
luck and nerves of steel to endure this bloodcurdling
adventure.

Armada

Puzzlequest

MICHAEL HOLT

The name of the game is spy-catching. YOU are summoned to M Fifteen, the famous espionage headquarters, by its ice-cold head of operations, N. Your mission is to foil the evil plans of Master Spy Count Jugula and his bungling accomplices, Amadeus, Wolffang and Mozart – code-named the Mozart Trio.

At critical stages of your journey you will be required to solve ingenious puzzles before you can continue your quest. Your trusty mongrel, Mugs, will accompany you. Together you make a dynamic duo as you struggle to win THE GREAT SPY RACE and unravel THE RIDDLE OF THE SPHINX.

Armada